DANCING TO PAY THE LIGHT BILL

DANCING TO PAY THE LIGHT BILL

Essays on New Mexico and the Southwest

Jim Sagel

R · E · D
CRANE
BOOKS

SANTA FE

First Edition

Printed in the United States of America

Cover and text design by Paulette Livers Lambert

Cover and text illustrations by Greg Tucker

Library of Congress Cataloging-in-Publication Data
Sagel, Jim.
  Dancing to pay the light bill : essays on New Mexico and the
Southwest / by Jim Sagel.—1st ed.
    p.   cm.
  ISBN 1-878610-10-4
  1. New Mexico—History, Local.   2. Southwest, New—History, Local.
3. New Mexico—Social life and customs.   4. Southwest, New—Social
life and customs.   I. Title.
F801.2.S24   1991
978.9—dc20   91-61531
                                                                                    CIP

Red Crane Books
826 Camino de Monte Rey
Santa Fe, New Mexico 87501

for Larry, Barbaraellen, y los ancianos del Norte

CONTENTS

ESSAYS

PREFACE

Shortly after my arrival in New Mexico more than twenty years ago, I came to realize that the most "enchanting" things about this land are not the wind-chiseled mesas and grandfatherly mountains, but the people who inhabit them. A sense of history permeates the everyday life of even the most assimilated *nuevomexicano*. Memories are long in this place where oral tradition is still alive in the stories swapped at the local post office and passed down through the generations over the kitchen table. The stamp of that oral tradition is on these essays as, indeed, it is on all of my work. No matter how serious the subject, I always find myself tempted to "dance" a bit, for, as Liberato Montoya knew so well, it is good humor that provides the light between the inevitable bills.

Over the past decade, I've worked to pay my light bill by writing portraits based on interviews I've conducted for the *Albuquerque Journal North*, *New Mexico* magazine, and other publications. However, truth be told, the interviews were principally for my own delight and ongoing education, as I sought out the *ancianos*, the elders of the Hispanic, Native American, Anglo-American, and black cultures of New Mexico. From century-old priests to saint-carving leaders of one-man bands, the individuals represented here have unique stories to tell, stories rich with humor and ripe with cultural history, stories that in their totality create a sense of the multicultural fabric that is the true beauty of this magical land.

Many of my friends who tell about their lives in the following pages have now died, but their wisdom, like the culture of New Mexico, lives on.

The Spanish I have used in writing these essays and portraits is the *español* of northern New Mexico, a dialect with several unique features. Among these are: archaic terms dating from the sixteenth and seventeenth centuries, the use of which has persisted due to the geographic isolation of New Mexico; words of indigenous origin, from the Nahuatl of the Aztecs to the Tewa of the Pueblo Indians; and, finally, bilingual anglicisms deriving from English, *caló* vocabulary (the code language developed by *pachucos*), and terms of local origin.

For further information on this unique variety of Spanish, the reader may refer to Rubén Cobos, *A Dictionary of New Mexico and Southern Colorado Spanish* (Santa Fe: Museum of New Mexico Press, 1983).

ACKNOWLEDGMENTS

The following original sources have given their consent for Red Crane Books to publish these essays and portraits in a revised form.

Albuquerque Journal, Journal North, and *Impact* Magazine:
"What If Kearny Had Taken the Wrong Turn at Las Vegas?"
"Invasion of the Greenbacks"
"One Percent for Etiquette"
"Lowdown Laughs: The Española Joke"
"The Blackout of '84"
" 'La Española' "
"Liberato Montoya"
"Sostenes Trujillo"
"Max Trujillo"
"Florence Naranjo"
"Father José Teres"
"Marcos Gómez"
"Anna Sopyn"
"Paul Pacheco"
"Reid Evans"
"Agueda Martínez"
"Peter García"
"Alfonso Alderete"
"Jenny Vincent"
"Patricio Cruz"
"Jesús Ríos"

New Mexico Magazine:
"¿Cómo se dice 'Big Mac' en español?: The Cultural Dynamics of 'Spanglish' "
"La Gallina de arriba: Los Dichos de la gente"
"Vamos por leña: The Rites of Autumn"
"La Comadre Sebastiana"
"Real New Mexicans Don't Eat Green Chile Quiche"

New Mexico Endowment for the Humanities and *The Santa Fe New Mexican:*
"Education and Other Little Known Dangers"

This essay appears courtesy of Sunstone Press, Box 2321, Santa Fe, New Mexico 87504-2321:
"El Turco: A Historical Monologue"

ESSAYS

I ♦

LOS DICHOS
DE LA GENTE
The Cultural Voice

¿CÓMO SE DICE "BIG MAC" EN ESPAÑOL?

The Cultural Dynamics of "Spanglish"

on Ramón no hace enjoy en los restaurantes. He'd rather eat at home, even if it's only *frijoles viejos y tortillas duras.* But it's Father's Day, and all of the *familia* is taking him out for dinner at Red's Steakhouse. So don Ramón is dressing up and he's going because, as doña Clotilde says, *"Más que no love it, él va a ir."*

Pero, más que no love it, don Ramón y doña Clotilde arrive bien tarde at Red's porque el carro está liquiando aceite, and don Ramón has to add a quart of Ward's All-Season 10-40, but he gets his *calzones puercos* in the process and has to go back inside the *casa a cambiar.* Then, on the way to the restaurant *don Ramón y doña Clotilde encuentran un roadblock en el highway, y tienen que hacer detour. Pronto pierden el way,* and before they know it the couple ends up stuck behind a long *caravana* of lowriders *tirando el cruise por el main drag. Al fin,* don Ramón is able to *meterse* into the left-hand turn lane, but he doesn't put his *brecas* in time *y—¡zaz!—se requea con una troca Ford.* By the time the *chotas* fill out their *reporte* and allow don Ramón and doña Clotilde to drive away in their battered car with the right fender *bien tuistiado,* Red's has already closed, and the members of the family have all gone back to the *chante.* So don Ramón and doña Clotilde pull into McDonald's *a comerse un Big Mac.*

Now you know the *triste historia* of don Ramón's and doña Clotilde's Father's Day adventures, but the question still remains: *¿Cómo se dice "Big Mac" en español?*

It is a question because certain individuals would cringe at the language used in the preceding *cuento*, perjoratively terming it "Spanglish." Such code-switching between English and Spanish, these linguistic purists warn, bastardizes both *lenguajes* and renders its users doubly illiterate.

But this narrow view ignores the fact that there are cultural and historical reasons for speaking "Spanglish," reasons reflected in the old *dicho*, *"Pobre México, tan lejos de Dios y tan cerca de los Estados Unidos*—Poor Mexico, so far from God and so close to the United States." Of course, for *nuevomexicanos* and other residents of the *Sudoeste*, it's not only "close to," but "part of." Which is why doña Clotilde sometimes begins her prayers by saying, *"Oh Dios, aquel de allá, porque el de aquí es americano."*

The linguistic impact of living more than a *siglo* under the eagle eye of *el dios americano* has been pervasive. New Mexicans, for instance, never learned to eat an *emparedado* while sitting beside the *alberca, pero sí podemos comernos un sandwich sentados juntos al swimming pool*. When we entered the first grade at school, we sat at a *desque* and sharpened our pencils in a pencil sharpener because our English-speaking *maestros* had never heard of a *tajalápices*, and by the time we entered high school and began typing our term papers, *los taipiamos en un typewriter* because no one had ever called it *una máquina de escribir*. When we drove our first Model T and shifted into third, we stepped on the *clotche*, not *el pedal del embrague*, and when we got back home, we never would have figured out how to *estacionar el coche*, but we sure knew how to *parquear el carro*.

Yet, "Spanglish" is not solely the result of the acquisition of English terminology to describe modern and technical phenomena. Otherwise, why would don Ramón have asked doña Clotilde to help him push their car away from the scene of the accident by saying, *"púshalo,"* when he could just as easily have said, *"empújalo"*? The two words, of course, have identical denotations, but the funky sound of *púshalo* evokes a totally different mood and effect.

The bilingual speaker is like a *pintor* with two sets of *colores*. He can utilize that expanded palette to introduce a variety of tones into his utterances. *Por ejemplo*, when doña Clotilde informed don Ramón that their *vecino* had died, his reaction to her was, *"Lástima que se murió el pobre."* But, later that same day when he ran into his *primo comprando sandpaper en la casa de Cooks*, don Ramón said,

"Pus, ya el vecino colgó los tenis." *La misma realidad*, but the "Spanglish" version imparts a different tone and attitude about death.

En otra ocasión, don Ramón was telling his *nieto* about what a strong and powerful man his own father had been, about how he was the one who had opened up that first road into the mountains with a team of *bueyes*, and about how he was still breaking wild horses when he died in his seventies. *"Mi papá era un hombre de verdad,"* don Ramón said to his grandson, *"no un 'sample' como yo."* It was no coincidence that don Ramón chose the English word *sample* to refer to his own diminished strength and status in a modern society dominated by a mass culture his father never could have imagined.

Though don Ramón is becoming increasingly bilingual, it is the younger generation that has made "Spanglish" their own, transforming the playful linguistic *baile* of code-switching into a veritable code-language of their own. *Y, ¿por qué no?*

It is, after all, the *jóvenes* who find themselves on the front lines of cultural upheaval. Born into a generation nurtured in front of a television, the young Hispanic must somehow sort out where his grandfather fits into the computer program. Must he, too, look, think, and act like all the homogenized *gente* in the McDonald's commercials, or can he retain some of his personal and ethnic *identidad*, even while chomping down on his own Big Mac?

It's "Spanglish" that allows the young Hispanic to bridge the two *mundos* of his daily existence, keeping him afloat in contemporary society and, yet, in touch with his *raíces*. When the "Spanglish" speaker says, *"Ahí te guacho,"* he is, indeed, using a word derived from English, but the utterance expresses his cultural identity more profoundly than, "See ya later."

Still, there are those who would fault don Ramón, not for failing to use his *brecas* in time, but for not understanding that it was his *frenos* and not his *brecas* that he failed to apply. And there are those who would criticize doña Clotilde for speaking "bad Spanish" when she said, *"Quiero un Big Mac."* But what do these pure-talking folks say when they sidle up to the counter to place their own orders: *"Deseo una hamburguesa Maque Grande"*?

The linguistic doomsayers may weep in their *diccionarios* all they want: they cannot stop the spread of "Spanglish." For all language is quicksilver, a constantly evolving mirror of reality. As long as the southwestern *espejo* reflects two cultural systems in daily collision and collusion, people will speak bilingually. *Más que no love it*, as doña Clotilde would say, ''Spanglish'' is here to stay.

LA GALLINA DE ARRIBA
Los Dichos de la gente

o every thing there is a season, and a time to every purpose under the heaven," declares the writer of Ecclesiastes. But had the wise old Hebrew scholar rented an adobe studio up in the Jémez Mountains to pen his biblical verses, he might have added, "And there's probably a *dicho* for every damn thing under the heaven, too."

For there is.

In the four centuries since Spanish-speaking settlers populated this arid land punctuated with fertile river valleys and rugged mountain ranges, a rich oral tradition has developed. One of the most concise and popular components of that storytelling tradition is the *dicho*, the carefully crafted saying that has been passed on from mouth to mouth and generation to generation with its wit and wisdom capsulated in a few well-chosen words.

The old ones of the Hispanic Southwest are the keepers of the *dichos*, and many of them can scarcely complete a sentence without remembering a particularly fitting *dicho* that their *tía* Gertrudes used to say or a wry adage that their *compadre* Teófilo always used when such a situation arose.

It would be a mistake to confuse the *dicho* with its stodgy cousin, the moralistic proverb. The proverb limps along on a stilted crutch, while the *dicho* pirouettes on a linguistic pogo stick. What's more, there was no Benjamin Franklin around to stultify the Spanish *dicho* in a dime store almanac—what's kept the *dicho* so vital is its oral nature.

And its irony. The essence of the *dicho* is its playful, often ironic tone; wit is the basic ingredient of the *dicho's* penetrating wisdom.

"*La gallina de arriba siempre caga en la de abajo*," one of my personal favorites, expresses a timeless reality in a sharp metaphor: "The top chicken always defecates on the one below."

And why does God allow such inequality to go unchecked throughout history? The *dichos* do not speculate on the motives of the Almighty, though they do characterize the incomprehensible workings of Providence in such concise terms as these: "*Dios da almendras al que no tiene muelas*—God gives almonds to those without any teeth."

Those with more teeth in their mouths than nickels in their pockets will encounter no strident denunciation of the upper classes in the *dichos*; they will, however, enjoy a good, self-effacing laugh at such reflections as: "*No es desgracia ser pobre, pero es muy inconveniente*—It's no disgrace to be poor, but it is very inconvenient."

It also can be awfully inconvenient to go through life stuck with an ugly face. "*¡Pobrecitos los feos si no hubiera malos gustos!*"—a *dicho* declares—"Pity the ugly if it weren't for bad taste!"

But what can a man do about the circumstances of his birth for, as a *dicho* puts it, "*Unos nacen con estrella y otros nacen estrellados*—Some are born under a star while others are born seeing stars."

Whether "under a star" or "seeing stars," most of the people of the past were born into a stark and difficult existence. And much of the pithy and often satiric wisdom of the *dichos* is an outgrowth of the gritty, subsistence lifestyle of the early residents of the frontier.

Thus, one encounters little moral posing in the *dichos*—none, to my knowledge, begins with the words "thou shalt not." In place of broad precepts, the *dichos* lend pointed advice on how to simply survive: in spite of the fact that Catholicism is a way of life as well as a religion in the Southwest, the *dichos* generally offer more tips on how to save one's skin than one's soul.

"*Primero es comer que ser cristiano*," says a *dicho*—"Eating comes before being a Christian." And when you do get the chance to eat, a *dicho* advises, by all means take full advantage of the opportunity. "*Hazte el tonto y come con las dos manos*—Pretend you're a fool and eat with both hands."

However, one should not be a fool when it comes to matters of life and death. "*De morir yo y que se muera mi abuela, que se muera mi abuela que es más viejita*—If it comes down to me dying or my grandma dying, let my grandma die because she's a lot older."

And when death, *la Comadre Sebastiana*, finally does usher *abuelita* off this sad stage of existence, one should not wallow in endless mourning. *"¡El muerto al pozo y el vivo al retozo!,"* a *dicho* crisply exhorts—"The dead to his hole and let the good times roll!"

A good number of the *dichos* are about the process of socialization, providing pointers on how to coexist with other members of the community. Interestingly, and perhaps inevitably, it is these *dichos* that tend to be the thorniest. *"De los parientes y el sol, entre más lejos, mejor,"* one *dicho* proclaims—"When it comes to relatives and the sun, the farther away they are, the better."

At times, another *dicho* observes, it would be preferable if the neighbors were also as far away as the sun. *"Muy buenas son las vecinas, pero me faltan tres gallinas*—The neighbor ladies are very nice, but I'm missing three chickens."

Marriage receives a particularly acid treatment in the *dichos*, originally created, one imagines, by married folks. *"Quien no tiene suegra ni cuñado es bien casado*—He who has neither mother-in-law nor brother-in-law is well married."

Another *dicho* puts it more directly: *"Te casaste, te fregaste*—You get married and you're done for."

The well-versed storyteller often uses *dichos* as a kind of running psychological commentary on the foibles of human behavior. *"De médico, poeta y loco, todos tenemos un poco,"* a *dicho* sagely notes—"We all have a bit of the doctor, the poet, and the madman within us."

And yet, another *dicho* advises, there is no accounting for the vast differences between us. *"Cada cabeza es un mundo,"* goes the saying reserved for those moments when one dismisses another's beliefs as hopelessly absurd—"Each head is a world unto itself."

The body of existing *dichos* is replete with such insightful reflections. *"Amor de lejos es para los pendejos,"* counsels one—"Love from afar is for fools." Yet, sometimes you can't even convince someone that you love them at close range, for, *"El peor sordo es el que no quiere oír*—There is no one deafer than he who does not wish to hear."

A dutiful mirror of daily reality, the *dichos* reflect the ambiguity of existence by sometimes offering contradictory advice.

"Aunque la mona se viste de seda, mona se queda," declares a *dicho*—"Even though the monkey dresses up in silk, she's still a monkey."

Yet, another *dicho* seems to suggest that clothes do, indeed, make the woman: "*Compuesta, no hay mujer fea*—Made up, there is no such thing as an ugly woman."

And what greater contrast than that between two *dichos* commenting on the question of whether one really gains wisdom with age?

"*El diablo lo que sabe es por viejo y no por diablo,*" notes one *dicho*— "The devil knows what he knows because of his experience and not because he's the devil." But another *dicho* quips, "*Entre más viejo, más pendejo*—The older you get, the more stupid you become."

"*Los dichos de los viejitos son evangelios chiquitos,*" a *dicho* about *dichos* observes—"The sayings of the old ones are like little gospels." For centuries, these "little gospels" have transmitted the values and spirit of a people. But as the old storytellers die out and the younger listeners lose their native language, the *dichos* are increasingly becoming more the realm of folklorists than folks.

Someday we may know the *dichos* only through anthologies on library shelves, as sayings that have been indexed for easy reference but that have little relevance to our lives. Maybe then we will realize what the *ancianos* meant when they said, "*No echamos de menos al agua hasta que se seca la noria*—We don't miss the water until the well runs dry."

VAMOS POR LEÑA
The Rites of Autumn

t's still hitting ninety by noon, and the apples are only beginning to blush; but the change is coming. The sap in the *álamos* is making a lazy U-turn; ants are working time and a half. That yellow speck on the horizon is not the rising sun but a school bus: it must be time to go for firewood.

Leña. The word itself sounds as crisp as the blow of an ax, as truncated as fall. At this time of year "*vamos por leña*" are the words on the tips of the tongues of *nuevomexicanos* from Tres Piedras down to Tecolote.

You might make it through the summer without building that obligatory adobe addition, and you could even slip by without planting a garden, but if you live in New Mexico, you must go for *leña*—it's one of those essential rituals.

Exhaustive preparations are necessary to participate in this ritual. You must borrow the neighbor's compressor to inflate your balding *llantas*, having already balanced your checkbook and discovered you can't even afford to buy a new pair of decent work gloves, much less a set of retreads to go bouncing off the razorback rocks and oil pan-splitting stumps on the mountain trails that the U.S. Forest Service euphemistically calls roads.

Then, you must clean last year's muck out of your Stihl Farmboss, mix gas, add oil, and sharpen the snub-nosed chain that your neighbor must have ruined last winter when you loaned him your *serruche*. Chances are you'll put the chain on backwards and have to take the saw apart again in the *monte*, but aggravation is an inevitable part of the ritual.

Which is why you make sure to throw in at least a couple of sixes of Buckhorn beer when you pack your lunch of boiled eggs and Spam. You're going to need it when you stand in line for your woodcutting permit.

Waiting in line is the inescapable opening round of the firewood ritual these days. As little as fifteen years ago, there were no lines for *permisos*. In fact, with all the butane addicts in the state, one was lucky to find another woodcutter on the entire mesa to give you a jump when the *batería* in your truck went dead. Thirty years ago, *nuevomexicanos* didn't even bother with permits, and fifty years ago, one simply hitched up the horse and took the wagon up the hill behind the house.

One might expect the *ancianos* who have lived through all those changes to be the most nervous members of the line that snakes all the way from the U.S. Forest Service gate down the hill to the highway. But the opposite seems true.

Two aging *compadres* stand in front of me at the Coyote district office. Though we arrived here in the dark, there were already at least a hundred more determined woodcutters ahead of us, including the true fanatics who camped out at Smokey's doorstep in sleeping bags. But the *compadres* continue to exchange their Lucky Strikes, talking in low, calm tones, just as they have for the last five hours, touching on every topic under the New Mexican sun, from the exorbitant price of baling wire to the fact that they both prefer those little native white *duraznos* to the bigger yellow peaches because they're sweeter, at least the way their wives can them.

Behind me a group of five young *batos* are getting *agüitados* with the long wait, nervously shifting from one foot to the other in an unconscious dance, running out of things to say now that they've discussed how one guy is replacing the tranny in his Mustang while the other is currently *sandeando su Chevy*, getting the '67 set for its fourteenth paint job in the last four years.

But, at long last, the line inches you into the inner sanctum, where you exchange a twenty-spot for a permit stipulating that you have only two weekends to withdraw your two cords of wood, which wouldn't be so bad except that there is an unwritten law of nature which dictates that it will invariably rain during the wood gathering season.

So you wallow through the mire of low-lying arroyos, struggling up the mountain in two-foot-deep ruts cut by four-wheel drives. You make sure your magnetized St. Christopher is securely in place on the dashboard, for if you meet a *troca* coming from the opposite direction on the narrow, rocky incline, you may have to back up a quarter of a mile or risk rolling down the side of a muddy precipice.

One thing you can dispense with, however, is the map. You hardly need to even watch the signs. The cacophony created by a school of chain saws buzzing simultaneously will announce your arrival at the firewood cutting block. You pass by trucks of every size, shape, and condition as you search for a place to cut. Yet, in spite of the competition, woodcutters tend to be friendly and gregarious: everybody waves. "*Llevas muy buena carga*—You've got a good load there," a *viejito* in a work shirt, suspenders, and rotting straw hat grins as you roll down the mesa, your overloaded truck a lurching, groaning dinosaur.

But even if you manage to get that "good load" home without blowing a tire or snapping an axle, you must never calculate what it cost you to bring down your quota of precious piñon, for once you've added up what you paid for the beer, gas, oil, lunch, permit, chain saw repair, and more beer, you'll probably realize it would have been cheaper to have stayed home and purchased the wood.

Of course, then you would not have participated in the ritual and received all the benefits that only the ritual can provide. One is the sense of belonging to a community, for, like all true rituals, woodcutting is at once communal and utterly private. There is a camaraderie among the members of the temporary woodcutting community, and yet there is a delicious solitude in the midst of the din.

It is a solitude made up of sights, sounds, and smells. The pungent scent of the crushed *chamisos* mingles with the incense of *trementina*—the piñon pitch. Tails of blue steam from your coffee thermos lick through the twisted branches of the *sabinos*. Sweat washes into your eyes, but when you blink them, you see the brilliant Jémez sky punctuated by the lofty tips of the ponderosas.

Rituals are also bound up in tradition, and there are few practices in New Mexico with a longer history than woodcutting. Of course, it was once necessary for survival. Now, woodcutting is more of a stubborn adherence to form, the ritualization of subsistence.

The major function of a ritual, though, is the contribution it makes to one's sense of identity. People perform a given rite because it helps define who they are. And that is really the bottom line in this woodcutting business. *Nuevomexicanos* cut their own *leña* because it is simply something that *nuevomexicanos* do—there is no other way to explain it.

Woodcutting, though, is a ritual in the throes of considerable change. The increasing popularity of wood heat and the endemic hang-up we have on piñon have led to such overharvesting of the wood that one old-timer told me, "In a few years, we're going to be crawling up the hills to collect cactus to burn."

The problem is compounded by wasteful cutters, a new and unscrupulous breed of wood gatherer who takes only the large blocks from the *pinos*, leaving the majority of the *leña* to rot on the forest floor. Notwithstanding numerous U.S. Forest Service regulations, these wood hogs leave the area looking like a bomb has hit, with slash impaled ten feet high and stumps standing as tall as a man.

When one considers the fact that it takes a hundred years or so to grow a good-size piñon tree, it doesn't take a seer to predict that the New Mexican woodcutting ritual, which has survived for hundreds of years, may disappear before this century ends.

LA COMADRE SEBASTIANA

n Spanish she's known by many names: *la Flaca* (the Skinny One), *la Huesuda* (the Bony One), *la Hedionda* (the Foul-Smelling One), or simply *la Muerte*. In New Mexico, she's *la Comadre Sebastiana*, the walking, talking, skeletal personification of death.

Though some are repulsed or at least baffled by what they consider a morbid preoccupation with death in Hispanic culture, they are dead wrong. *La Comadre Sebastiana* is anything but morbid. In the popular stories and communal imagination, the figure of Death is one of the liveliest, spiciest, and most downright humorous characters imaginable.

Part of the reason for *la Comadre Sebastiana's* poor image in some quarters may stem from her identification with the terrifying figures carved by New Mexican *santeros,* principally for use in the *carretas de muerte,* or death carts, found in Penitente *moradas.* These wooden skeletons of Death are typically carved holding a hatchet or the bow and arrow of mortality, and they are truly foreboding. But, then, they are intended to be, and intention is the key difference between the *Muerte* of the death cart and that of the traditional stories. The death cart figure, after all, is meant to inspire fearful contemplation of one's own mortality, to focus the mind of the Penitente *hermano* on the pain and suffering of Christ.

Quite a different figure of Death creaks into the traditional *cuentos,* or stories. This *Muerte* is more likely to make you howl with laughter than fear, for the primary purpose of the stories is to entertain. Of course, the *cuentos* almost always are didactic as well; there is a "moral" to every story, which transmits a historical truth or cultural value, or, as is often the case, pokes fun at human foibles.

Take, for instance, the well-known story in the Hispanic oral tradition of *los dos viejos quejándose*—the two old people who were complaining. The elderly couple was complaining, it seems, about their aches and pains, and before long they had entered into a kind of competition of earthly woes. "*Estoy tan enfermo*—I'm so sick," said the old man, "that I wish I could just die."

"*¡Tú no tienes nada!*" the ancient woman responded. "You are not so sick! Look at me—half blind and all crippled with arthritis. *I'm* the one who ought to die!"

And so they carried on until *la Comadre Sebastiana* arrived to announce that she had come for one of them. "Take her!" the old man said.

"No! Take him!" the woman cried. "He's *much* sicker than I am!"

In a good number of the stories about *la Comadre Sebastiana*, the humor turns on her very human character flaw of gullibility. *La Muerte* gets tricked an awful lot, especially by one Pedro de Ordimalas or Urdemales—he goes by many aliases, but he's always the same old *pícaro*, the familiar rogue of Hispanic folklore and literature who lives (and sometimes dies) by his wits. Time and again, Pedro tricks *la Comadre Sebastiana* into giving him a little more time, whether it's with a magic tree, an enchanted drum, or a wonderful chair that keeps its user stuck for a century.

The humor, of course, is black by most people's standards— certainly, it is ironic, for Death in the stories, as in real life, always wins in the end. Yet, often it is that very ending, that final twist of fate, that evokes the heartiest laughter. A case in point is one of my personal favorites, the *cuento* about the recently married couple who is sharing breakfast one fine New Mexican morning when *la Comadre Sebastiana* comes rolling up to the door. "Pedro!" she calls—"I have come for your soul!"

Needless to say, Pedro is rather set on holding onto his soul for a little while longer, and so he begins to think fast (as the Pedros in the oral tradition are wont to do). "*Préstame las tijeras*," he tells his wife—"Lend me the scissors. I'm going to cut off all my hair. Maybe that way Death won't recognize me."

Dicho y hecho—said and done, as they say. Meanwhile, *la Comadre Sebastiana*, who, naturally enough, never waits to be invited in, has entered the house and demands to know where Pedro is. "*No está aquí*," his wife stutters at the sight of the fleshless hag—"He's not here."

"*¿Cuándo regresa?*" Death asks.

"I don't know when he'll be back. He didn't say—probably not for a long time."

"*Bueno*," *la Comadre Sebastiana* says, pulling up a chair at the kitchen table. "I'll wait until he gets home."

After a while, Pedro comes out—he can't stay in the bedroom all day, after all—and he sits at the table with Death, who immediately hisses, "*¿Quién es?*"

"Oh—this is my...my father," Pedro's wife replies uncertainly. *Pero ¡qué maravilla!*—it's incredible, but Death appears to be fooled by Pedro's radical haircut, which has left him totally bald.

Well, to make what the traditional storytellers would render as a very long story short, *la Comadre Sebastiana* stays all day long, waiting for the return of the *alma* that is rightfully hers. At last, as the sun is about to set Death stands up and says: "I guess you're right, *mujer*. It looks like your husband isn't going to come. *¡Pero para no perder el viaje, me llevo a este pelado conmigo!*—But, so I don't waste the trip, I'll take this baldy here along with me!"

Now, what is the meaning of all this, you might ask. Frankly, I hesitate to discuss the significance of *la Comadre Sebastiana*, partly because the stories are so delightful they don't deserve philosophic dissection and partly because—well, knowing her ironic sense of humor, I wouldn't be surprised to hear her knobby knuckles rapping at my *own* door even while I'm in the process of expounding on her ironic sense of humor.

Nevertheless, there are some speculations one can make about our skeletal taxi driver to the beyond. The principal point relates to her personification, the feature that most distinguishes the Hispanic figure from the mainstream view of death as a kind of metaphysical cloud of carbon monoxide—colorless, odorless, invisible, and insidious, an entity (in the made-for-TV-movie sense of the word) to be mortally feared and battled to the death in intensive care units.

In the Hispanic tradition, Death is a flesh-and-bone character (missing, of course, the flesh), as anthropomorphic a figure as the Native American Coyote or Fox. Death's essential "humanity" relates, no doubt, to the long tradition of Catholicism in Hispanic New Mexico—not the institutional Catholicism of the church in Rome nor the equally "distant" French cathedral in Santa Fe—but the traditional New Mexican brand of Catholicism, crystallized over centuries of struggle on the frontier and maintained by an intense personal faith in this isolated land where there were precious few priests.

Here, God was no ethereal abstraction but, rather, a personal *Dios*, seen and revered in His personal form, the form of those austere wooden *santos* that still stand like sentinels in the churches, *capillas*, and *moradas* of the Southwest. There is a direct corollary in the *cuentos* in which the saints, especially San Pedro, come alive. There are even stories in which Jesucristo Himself walks through the piñon studded hills of New Mexico.

Thus, it is no surprise that *la Comadre Sebastiana* should come rattling into the stories for a little *atole* and repartee before doing her dirty deed. But there is an additional implication here that has to do with her humorous nature. Just as the rugged past generations bred in this northern frontier learned to rely on their *santos* and their faith in order to endure the frequent and inevitable hardships of life, so, too, they came to know the reality of death on intimate terms. A strong strain of fatalism evolved over the years, stemming in part, perhaps, from long-buried Islamic roots, and still reflected today in the anterooms of mortuaries and church parking lots throughout New Mexico, where one hears, "*Bueno, ya le tocaba*— Well, it was his time to go."

It would be a mistake, however, to associate this fatalistic orientation to death with a sense of despair or existential angst. Exactly the opposite is the case. Freely accepting the inevitability of death is a liberating experience—joyful even. It's something to joke about, deprecate oneself about, embrace like a lover, and love like life, for, ironically, it is precisely the acceptance of death that allows and motivates us to *live* our lives rather than postponing every passionate act and rescheduling every risky venture for a later date because we've tricked ourselves into believing we'll somehow live forever.

But we won't live forever—¡*gracias a Dios!* "¡*El muerto al pozo y el vivo al retozo!*"—as the old saying puts it—"The dead to his hole and let the good times roll!" ¡*Que viva la Comadre Sebastiana!*

II

MIMBRES TO MANHATTAN
The Historical Voice

EL TURCO
A Historical Monologue

oy el Turco. "The Turk" they call me, even though I've got no more Ottoman blood in my veins than your grandmother's Chihuahua. But those Spaniards—heads all mushed up with Moorish devils as they were—well, as soon as they got a load of my swarthy good looks, they labeled me "the Turk," and the nickname just stuck. But, then, I've never been to India either, and you all call me "Indian," so what's the difference?

Esclavo me llaman también—they call me "slave." But he who claims to own me is a greater slave than I. Didn't they chain up my so-called master, old Pecos Bigotes, when he dared to disagree with my tall tales? And, speaking of *bigotes,* who could imagine a more servile subject than the mighty *bigotón* himself, don Francisco Vásquez de Coronado, slave to my silvery tongue and the shimmering illusion of my gold-leafed words?

Sí, soy el embustero, one of history's great liars, but don't act so smug—I can still trick you too. So tell me, what do you want to hear? That's my skill, you see: I paint poems out of your dreams. I embellish the greedy underbelly of your fantasies, and the more fantastic my story, the easier it is to beguile you. You want to hear about that winning lottery ticket waiting for you at the 7 to 11 Speedway across from Colonel Sanders Kentucky Fried Chicken that has the exact numbers of the birth date, weight, and championship record of the "Manassa Mauler," Jack Dempsey? Or would you rather hear about the killing you could make in the stock market if you'd take an early retirement and cash in your insurance policies in order to get in on the ground floor of a new artificial spleen company with home offices located on the outskirts of Hoboken?

No se rían. Well, go ahead and laugh if you want, but I know my material works. After all, I've got more than four centuries of experience under my belt, and I know these are no fireside yarns. Feet follow my fictions—when I engage you in flights of fantasy, we're talking airline reservations on a 747 bound for Madagascar.

I mean, just consider that classic scam I ran on Coronado back in 1541. Poor *pendejo* was shivering that winter in the *pueblito* of Alcanfor, suffering from the symptoms of Cíbola Withdrawal Syndrome—I tell you he was ripe for a little "gold goading." So I invented Quivira, took it straight from his romantic medieval mind-set, and we may have been leagues off-Broadway, but, boy, did it play! Forget the Halls of Montezuma, I told Coronado. To the east lay an even golder kingdom—yes, the land of Quivira, where there was so much gold his troops would have to rent U-Hauls just to cart it all away. Oh yes, Quivira, where golden bells tinkled from the boughs of stately trees at the banks of a river six miles wide where royalty serenely floated in canoes with golden prows and sipped sweet wine from silver goblets.

Not bad for an amateur, no? Especially when you consider we're talking about Kansas here. Actually, I may have waxed a little too eloquently for, come spring, I was out there myself, leading Coronado and the boys down the trail to Quivira, which called for some pretty fancy improvisation on the old "just over the next hill" theme. The history books, of course, will tell you they executed me out there on the "lone prairie," but don't you believe it for a minute. They couldn't kill me, not so long as there was a steady supply of new fools eager to tilt at gilded windmills.

Fifty years later, I was at it again, resurrecting tales of golden wonder and sending Captain Francisco Leyva de Bonilla thundering off into the sunrise. That time, I'll admit, I did accept a little kickback from the residents of San Ildefonso Pueblo, who had gotten sick and tired of maintaining the Spaniard on their welfare rolls. Leyva, of course, never came back, but that's not my problem—I just weave the stories and say good-bye. I even said *adiós* to your famous colonizer Juan de Oñate when I seduced him out of his happy new home at San Gabriel and right back down that same trail through the buffalo chips and the greasy grass. By then they were calling me Jusepe or José or just plain old Joe—but it was really me, *el Turco.*

Todavía sigo mintiendo—and why shouldn't I keep on lying, seeing as how there are more *locos* than ever these days, people who want to believe their fantasies are true because they are too blind to see how fantastic the truth really is. Do you follow me? Better not, or I'll lure you away from the river valley, too. I'll snatch you from the snowy arms of the mountains and everything that's important to you and set you trudging through the empty grasslands of your heart, where the horizon is endless and the future is flat and there are no directions back home.

For I am the cave without a mouth, the splash of sunlight blazing adobe walls into golden fortresses. I am the rain refusing to rain. I crash anthropologists' cocktail parties and plant corn by night in the lawns of chiropracters. I play recordings of *la Llorona* weeping in the *bosque* where the Río Chama flows into the Río Grande. I built Georgia O'Keeffe's wall, and I was responsible for Article VIII of the Treaty of Guadalupe Hidalgo, for all that was worth. I only wish I had never made up that insane story I told to J. Robert Oppenheimer because I'll be damned if that one didn't turn out to be true! I'm still busy today, convincing the heirs of Oñate and Popé to become professional basketball players, and I'm packing them into the Coronado Mall with visions of bigger and better Quiviras dancing in their heads.

¿Qué dicen?—that I have the scruples of a cow stomach? Well, perhaps you haven't heard the old *dicho: "El que le roba a un ladrón tiene cien años de perdón*—He who steals from a thief is pardoned for a hundred years." My tales lead no man where he has not already decided to go. I stay here, at the banks of my beloved *río,* in the embrace of my timeless pueblo, spinning stories that simply drive the driven on by. Only problem is lately I've been stumped by all these condominium developers, who scoff at my easterly stories and sniff that they've already subdivided Quivira Estates. If anyone can come up with a story idea brazen enough to mesmerize this new breed of colonizers, I'd sure appreciate hearing it.

Mientras tanto, I'll keep searching for my favorite listeners, those who turn a deaf ear to each other. Give me those hard and intolerant men of lofty righteousness, those who pray by rote and never question the king, the men who really want to get ahead in life. As long as I have breath and wits, I'll keep making up my outrageous stories to urge them farther on, far away from my peaceful home by the river.

WHAT IF KEARNY HAD TAKEN THE WRONG TURN AT LAS VEGAS?

 film about a time machine evokes an ageless human curiosity: how might the present be altered if some significant event in the past were changed?

Nowhere could that curiosity be keener than in New Mexico, a land that has felt the bare foot of the Anasazi and the hiking boot of the New Buffalo hippie, a land etched with the conquistador's horseshoe and the crater of the first nuclear blast, a state whose destiny has been shaped by conquests, connivances, contrivances, and still more conquests.

But what if the famous reconquest of New Mexico in 1692 had never occurred? What if don Diego de Vargas, horrified by the tales of Otermín, had decided to stay home in his split-level ranch house with the two-*caballo* garage on the *zócalo* in Mexico City, perfectly content to let the Indians keep that godforsaken north land?

If the reconquest of New Mexico had never taken place following the Pueblo Revolt, today all New Mexicans, or "Anasazians," as we'd be called, would look not to the pope in Rome for spiritual guidance, but, rather, to the Popé in San Juan Pueblo. His word would be law over the length and breadth of "Oweenge," as our sovereign nation would be known.

There would be no strip mines in Oweenge and no Army Corps of Engineers interfering with the timeless flow of the rivers. Those caught poaching or littering in the Great Tewa Forest would be sentenced to two years of hard bingo labor, distributing cards and selling Cokes in the huge bingo coliseums.

Repeat offenders would be compelled to paint license plates with the words, "Oweenge is OK," which would be the official national motto after Popé XII successfully petitioned the U.S. government to force Oklahoma to drop the slogan because Oweenge had prior rights to it since time immemorial.

Less serious offenses and minor civil suits would be tried in the local kivas, which means, of course, that Reies López Tijerina never would have gained prominence because it would have been impossible to raid a county courthouse with only a single hole in the roof for an entrance.

But what if Tijerina had not only captured the Tierra Amarilla Courthouse in 1967, but actually kept it when hundreds, then thousands of ranchers rallied to his support? With all the publicity generated for his cause, Tijerina might have convinced Willie Nelson and Julio Iglesias to throw a land grant benefit, a "Mercedes Aid" concert. Though many of the well-heeled concert-goers would have believed the benefit was on behalf of their car manufacturer, the money would have been used to purchase enough kerosene to torch every National Forest Service sign from Costilla down to Columbus.

Of course, all those pyrotechnics might never have been necessary had it not been for J. Robert Oppenheimer's passion for pines. Imagine the consequences had the brilliant young scientist never been to the boys' school tucked away in the Jémez Mountains, thinking, as many Americans still do today, that New Mexico was a part of Mexico.

If "Oppie" had set up shop, say, in the Ozarks, the unemployment rate in northern New Mexico today would be twice as high, though people might actually eat better, forgoing frozen pizza and Stove Top stuffing for the *chicos* and chile grown in their gardens. And grandchildren might be able to speak to grandparents in their native tongue while they harvested that chile and corn grown on land that the elders would not have sold in the 1940s and 1950s in order to go to work in Los Alamos.

Naturally, much of that land was long gone before anyone realized that *E* equalled *mc²*, but that might not have been the case if Colonel Stephen Watts Kearny had misread the road map he picked up at Armijo's Exxon and taken the wrong turn at Las Vegas. The good colonel, soon to be general, would have ended up conquering the Oklahoma Panhandle, New Mexico would have remained a part of Mexico, and the 1848 Treaty of Guadalupe Hidalgo would have been nothing more than a bad dream.

Not only would Hispanics have been better off, retaining their traditional land grants issued by the Spanish Crown and the Mexican government, but many *gringos* would have benefited as well. Charles Bent up in Taos, for instance, would have been able to keep his hair on his head, for the trader never would have been appointed governor.

The Navajo Nation, likewise, would now be three times its current size and far more powerful, for there would have been no Kit Carson to round the "Diné" up in 1864 and march them off on the "Long Walk" to the Bosque Redondo. Fort Sumner, in fact, never would have been constructed inasmuch as General Carleton would have stayed bodysurfing out on the sun-splashed beaches of southern California.

Of course, there would have been thousands of additional American deaths in Japan during World War II because the U.S. would not have had the invaluable services of the Navajo "code-talkers," but, on the other hand, no New Mexicans would have died on that other death march in the Bataan Peninsula.

Those *nuevomexicanos* who did survive the war returned to their Sangre de Cristos, Sandías, and Sacramento Mountains to find an altered economy, one in which they could no longer make a subsistence living on their ranches, but part of the reason for that, of course, was the fact that the land base had been whittled away over the previous century. But imagine how that sad state of affairs might have been ameliorated had Thomas Benton Catron decided to go into the priesthood instead of real estate, saying mass instead of amassing three million acres of New Mexican land.

No doubt Catron's disarming charm and entrepreneurial drive would have sent him skyrocketing through the church hierarchy, especially if he had learned French instead of Spanish as his second language. He might even have succeeded Lamy when death finally came for the archbishop.

But what might Willa Cather have written had Rome heeded the advice of the territorial parishioners and named the popular scholar, educator, and Taos priest Antonio José Martínez as first bishop of the Archdiocese of Santa Fe instead of Jean Baptiste

Lamy? Though Cather might have entitled her famous novel *Death Comes Not a Moment Too Soon for the Licentious, Yellow-Toothed, So-Called Archbishop*, the mass of the New Mexican population would still be reaping the cultural benefits today. We'd still have the art treasures that Lamy found so primitive and reprehensible, the wooden *santos*, *reredos*, and *retablos*, so many of which ended up as ashes in the French prelate's fireplace.

Tourists might miss the picturesque spires of St. Francis Cathedral in the background of their snapshots, but the thick adobe walls and flat roof of Bishop Martínez's cathedral would have inspired a more profound spirituality, one built out of the materials of New Mexico's own cultural heritage.

But if you want to muse over the impact of history on architecture, consider what the State Roundhouse would look like today if the Spaniards had decided to leave the capital in its original location of San Gabriel, a few miles up the river from present-day Española. Shaped like a political pie with several slices missing, the Half-Roundhouse would be situated between Taco Bell and Mr. Cheese Pizza and would house a governor elected for a life term (or until his political clout eroded, whichever came first). All state vehicles would be lowered to within two inches of the pavement and would be equipped with a governor on the speedometer, which would prevent them from exceeding a speed of twenty-five miles per hour. The main topic of conversation over Tecates and Slim Jims at the posh Española Inn of the Governors would, of course, be those moronic Santa Fe jokes.

But it would have been no joke had Francisco Vásquez de Coronado realized back in 1540 that he was trampling right over the gold he was so desperately seeking. With his mind fueled by Fray Marcos de Niza's fabulous tales of the Seven Cities of Cíbola, Coronado kept his eyes glued on the horizon, hoping to catch the faintest glint of those golden walls.

But had he simply sunk his *pala* into the mountains at Cerrillos instead of wandering off through the grassy plains of Kansas in search of gilded fantasies, the historical impact would have been mind-boggling.

The first whiff of gold in those mountains would have set off a stampede north from Mexico City that would have made the California gold rush look like a Sunday afternoon cakewalk. King

Charles would have built a super highway across *la Jornada del Muerto* faster than Juan de Oñate could click his silver spurs together.

The legacy of the Great Spanish Gold Rush would have been urban sprawl all along the Río Chiquito, as we in latter-day generations would know the once great river. Subdivisions would have sprouted in the Sangre de Cristos, while adobe skyscrapers obscured Taos Mountain. D.H. Lawrence, no doubt, would have stayed in England; Georgia O'Keeffe never would have moved to New Mexico to get away from it all for it all would have been here.

As these historical reveries dead-end in nightmares, and Morenci skies dissolve into Pittsburgh grey, I think it's time to pinch our collective selves and thank whatever power resides beyond that unblemished sky that things turned out exactly as they did, for it's our tumultuous history that has made us what we are today, an eclectic and fiercely independent people living in this land of bittersweet enchantment.

GABRIEL'S BAR & GRILL
A Historical Fantasy

t was the strangest barroom brawl I had ever seen.

I was sitting in Gabriel's Bar & Grill, that new place on the west side, nursing my Bud Light and listening to the Seven Sisters of Cíbola on the jukebox when, all of a sudden, a fight broke out at the pool table.

"Hey, you scratched, sucker—that's the game!" shouted the Silver Kid. His real name was Juan de la O, from down in the south side barrio Zacateclas, but everyone knew him as the Silver Kid because of the silver earring he wore in his left ear, the silver studs on his black leather jacket, and the huge silver crucifix he always wore around his neck.

"*¡Tu madre!*" came the snarled reply from the Silver Kid's opponent, Popé. Though Popé was a Pueblo Indian who lived right across the river, he had hung around Chicanos long enough to pick up a few such choice Spanish epithets. Now, as the Silver Kid brandished his cue stick threateningly, a fire began to smolder in Popé's black eyes.

"Cough up that twenty-spot, *ése*," warned the Silver Kid as six of his *cuates* silently emerged from the shadows to surround him at the end of the table.

"You owe me more than that for all the times you cheated me out of games in the past," Popé replied as a half dozen of his own friends stepped forward to his end of the table, their faces chiseled and set.

"The past?" the Silver Kid crowed. "Man, you're *living* in the past. You ever notice that? It's all you ever talk about."

"Maybe that's because life was better before you moved into town and messed everything up. This used to be a nice, quiet place, you know."

"Oh, gimme a break, will you?" the Silver Kid grimaced. "So you forgot already who brought you that horse you cruise around town on? And what about that wool sweater you're wearing? Where you think that came from—J. C. Penney?"

"Sure—you brought sheep—and you brought smallpox and slavery too," Popé spat back. "More than a thousand years we've been coming to this bar—*we* were the first ones here. You've got no right to take it over and call it your own."

"Wait just a minute. I was in church last Sunday, and the priest was complaining about devil worship and idolatry going on in here—people dancing around in costumes and making heathen noises. That's why I brought along my bro Frankie to convert you all," the Silver Kid said, gesturing to a bony man at his side dressed up in overalls and a blue cassock.

"That's the one!" Popé growled in anger. "He's the one who had me thrown in jail for so-called witchcraft, even though it was *his* offense to the rain gods that brought on the terrible drought and famine."

"Hold on, brother," the Silver Kid said. "You weren't the only one who suffered. I ate my share of toasted cowhides back in '68, too."

"And so you will again!" Popé cried as he leapt over the table and fell upon the Silver Kid. In an instant, the bar was in an uproar as the opposing camps wrestled each other across the pool table and onto the floor.

"Haven't I kicked you out of this place before?" Popé said as he delivered a karate chop to the Kid's neck.

"Naw—you're thinking about that wimp Otermín," the Kid replied, thrusting his cue stick into Popé's left kidney.

"Break it up!" yelled the bartender, a brawny Black Muslim by the name of Steve. I had seen him break up many a fracas before, but I wondered whether this one hadn't gone too far even for Steve to handle when, suddenly, a cry came from some *bato* standing by the window.

"*¡Los Apaches!*" he shrieked.

All hostilities inside the bar immediately ceased. Enemies, who a moment before had been locked in mortal combat, now joined forces, upturning tables and chairs to barricade the door. I lent a hand, for I, too, knew the reputation of this marauding gang of toughs who pillaged the countryside in stolen cars, ripping off whatever they pleased. But an unexpected sight came to our eyes as we cringed behind the windows—the Apaches were retreating. Once the huge cloud of dust settled, we understood why. The Hell's Angels had arrived.

Our barricade snapped like a wall of matchsticks when the head Angel drove his Harley straight through the door. He was a hulking monster of a man, whose enormous rolls of fat strained at the seams of his army camouflage T-shirt. An American flag tattoo was visible on one hairy forearm—"Mother" was on the other. A bushy red beard hung halfway down his chest, and a ten-gallon Stetson was perched high on his shaggy head. It was Big Daddy Kearny, just come over the pass with his sweet mama, Kitty Carson.

"Drinks are on the house!" Steve the bartender declared in the anxious tone of a man who knows he's years away from paying off the mortgage.

"May. . . may we wash your motorcycle for you, Mr. Angel?" asked one of the Silver Kid's pals, a guy by the name of Armijo.

"The name's Kearny, and I don't need no carwash," the bearded giant thundered. "Check it out—everything's cool. We ain't gonna hurt nobody. We're just here to lay down the law, and from now on, you're all gonna follow it! Now, for all I care you can hang around here and get drunk every damn night, but don't you forget *I'm* the boss around here now, and what I say goes. Me and Kitty gonna split now and round up that Navajo gang, so don't do nothin' to cross me and you won't get into no trouble."

"By the way," Big Daddy Kearny said as he roared out the door, "from now on I control all the booze that flows through this joint. So if you wanna drink, you're gonna have to lay down your cue sticks and duke it out in court."

The drone of the motorcycles had scarcely abated when an army of lawyers began emerging from the woodwork. Some climbed out from behind the bar, others crawled out from under the tables—still others came trotting out of the restroom with bulging briefcases and towering stacks of legal documents for Popé and the Silver Kid to sign. Before long, the whole place was engulfed in a cacophony of legalese.

For the life of me, I couldn't make heads or tails out of any of it. The lawyers seemed to be arguing about whether Popé or the Kid had first rights to the alcohol served in the bar. Popé's lawyers claimed he had "*primacia* rights" to the liquor, while the Kid's *abogados* claimed the Treaty of Guadalupe Hidalgo guaranteed the "privatization" of all drinking rights, thereby and thereafter granting the Kid a fundamentally equal shot at the Schlitz.

It was all very confusing. The only thing I could be sure of was, for all the arguing over who got the booze, the lawyers were the only ones doing any drinking. The haggling and shouting at last grew so intolerable that Popé suddenly cried out, "Enough!"

"*¡Ya basta!*" echoed the Silver Kid as he reached into his ancient scabbard and withdrew his silver sword. Popé, likewise, untied the yucca cord knotted around his waist, and the pair drove the lawyers out of the bar.

Delirious with laughter, the Kid and Popé collapsed together on the floor. When the laughter subsided, a hush fell over Gabriel's Bar & Grill. The Silver Kid looked Popé in the eye and said, "We've been pretty stupid not to realize that we've got a lot more in common than our enemies."

"Yes," Popé replied, "our peoples are one."

"Bros?" said the Kid, extending his hand.

"Brothers," Popé said, receiving it.

III

GREENBACKS
AND GREEN
CHILE QUICHE
The Satirical Voice

REAL NEW MEXICANS DON'T EAT GREEN CHILE QUICHE

eal New Mexicans don't eat green chile quiche. Even if it comes with posole.

Only those trying too hard to be real New Mexicans insist on eating chile with every meal. Häagen-Dazs is not likely to increase its number of real New Mexican customers by serving jalapeño ice cream.

Real New Mexicans must, however, have their tortillas. In the absence of tortillas, real New Mexicans will flatten slices of Rainbo bread by slapping them between their palms. When forced to eat without tortillas, the real New Mexican finds himself unable to control his left hand, which twitches and flops like a rainbow trout at the perimeter of his plate.

Real New Mexicans are invariably self-employed. Even when working for a boss, they somehow seem to be working for themselves. When offered the choice, real New Mexicans will opt to be paid for their work in beef jerky rather than cash, but it is a malicious rumor that real New Mexicans mug their neighbors to get their piñon wood.

All real New Mexicans have a corral behind the house where they keep the two horses they never ride. Real New Mexicans also own no less than three pigs, a pair of foul-tempered German sheperds, a half-dozen chickens, and at least one kamikaze rooster.

Real New Mexicans do not curse lowriders, nor do they signal when executing a U-turn. On backroads, however, they wave religiously at every oncoming car: a flick of the forefinger for an acquaintance and a barely perceptible nod of the head at strangers.

Real New Mexicans never purchase new cars, especially those that require the use of metric tools to change the oil. Neither do real New Mexicans sell or trade in used cars. Next to the size of the firewood pile, there is no prouder sign of prosperity in the real New Mexican's yard than the number of cars up on blocks.

Real New Mexicans avoid such futile gestures as replacing shocks on their cars. On trips they always take a supply of baling wire to wire their mufflers back on. Of course, real New Mexicans rarely leave their homes in the first place, convinced, as they are, that they already live in the most wonderful place on earth. It is equally rare to find a real New Mexican who has a street address. Real New Mexicans always live at the end of the third driveway down the fourth arroyo past the big cottonwood after the second bridge over the river.

Even if a real New Mexican has been urbanized to such an extent that he actually has numbers over his door, he'll still tell you the best way to find his place is simply to stop anywhere and ask for directions because everyone in the area knows where he lives.

Real New Mexicans go to funerals, even if they didn't know the deceased. They are frequently found at wedding dances trying to bribe the band to keep on playing.

Real New Mexicans still call each other *comadre* and *compadre*. They abhor losing at cards.

Real New Mexicans have a couple of fireplaces they never use because they're so inefficient, but the real New Mexican would lop off the tops of his fence posts before putting out ninety bucks for a cord of wood, preferring, instead, to spend one hundred dollars for a tank of gas, a fuel wood permit, a box of Kentucky Fried Chicken, two six-packs of Bud, and a new chain for his chain saw in order to go up to the national forest to cut his own firewood.

Real New Mexicans sing along with the radio. If they don't own a guitar, they wish they did. As a rule, real New Mexicans work harder after they retire.

You can always pick out the real New Mexican living in a trailer court. He's the one who's built an adobe skirting around his mobile home.

Real New Mexicans never give up trying to transplant junipers. And they always look astonished when it rains.

Seven out of ten real New Mexicans do not own a wristwatch; eight out of ten forget to flip their calendars over every month. Nine out of ten real New Mexicans own a television set that has been broken for more than half a year.

Real New Mexicans never throw anything away. Trader Jack's Flea Market would fold if it weren't for real New Mexicans; several newspapers would go bankrupt without the revenue generated by classified ads announcing yard and garage sales.

Real New Mexicans are inordinately lucky at bingo. They make their own wine and remember the weather from fifteen years ago.

Real New Mexicans laugh a lot; most have pictures of their great-grandparents. Real New Mexicans are the ones in the theater who cheer at all the wrong places when watching westerns.

Anyone claiming to be a real New Mexican who does not grow his own squash and tomatoes is a sure imposter. The authenticity of real New Mexicans, in fact, may be judged by the volume of mud under their fingernails and on the soles of their boots.

Yet, the bottom line, the acid test for real "*nuevomexicanismo*" is quite simple. Just look for the person who could care less what a real New Mexican should be like.

That's him. Or her.

INVASION OF
THE GREENBACKS

et's face it: the immigration problem is out of control, in spite of the Immigration and Naturalization Act and the beefed-up INS. What is lacking in this ongoing battle, however, is not the resources nor the resolve. The problem, quite simply, is that we're chasing after the wrong people.

In New Mexico, the real immigration threat does not come from the south but, rather, the east and the west as wave after wave of well-heeled refugees from New York and California flood over our unguarded borders. These aliens pull into town in the dead of night, towing enormous trailers jammed with their worldly possessions. Before long, condo *barrios* sprout up on the mesas like malignant mushrooms.

There's no disputing the fact that we need these immigrants to harvest our annual crop of fine art, jewelry, and pottery. Yet, we cannot ignore the tremendous economic burden this human deluge imposes on New Mexico. Lines at automatic teller machines across the state have become intolerable. Hospitals are overcrowded with all those people who can actually afford to see a doctor.

Crime is rising, since there's so much more to steal, and our neighborhoods are going—literally. Demolition crews can't flatten landmark buildings fast enough in order to make room for the new galleries and boutiques.

Clearly, the time for action has come: We New Mexicans must regain control of our borders. For that reason, I suggest we adapt the national Immigration and Naturalization Act to our local circumstances in an attempt to restrict the onslaught of all these "greenbacks" pouring into town.

At the heart of the New Mexican Immigration and Naturalization Act would be strict "seller sanctions." Any property owners selling land to illegals would face stiff fines and possible prison terms. Obviously, we don't want to shut the door entirely, especially during the busy summer harvest months of tourism, so the legislation would call for special green Visa and Mastercards that would, of course, have stringent credit limits. Further, the bill would demonstrate our magnanimity by granting amnesty to all immigrants dwelling in New Mexico since (let's see, when did I arrive here?), say, 1969.

What's more, the new law would establish procedures whereby more recent immigrants could apply for legalization status. This special status would apply only to aliens who have been here since January 1, 1980, and would be contingent upon successful fulfillment of the following requirements:

All such applicants would need to have lived continuously in New Mexico (no jaunts to either coast) for three years. During that time, they must have abstained from planting a lawn, driving either of their BMWs, or building any shopping malls.

Moreover, at the end of the three-year term, they would be required to pass a special qualifying exam. Among other items, they would be asked to:

• Pick Georgia O'Keeffe out of a mug shot book of contemporary artists.

• Correctly pronounce the place-names of Tecolote, Picurís, Pojoaque, and Guachupangue.

• Know the names of all the children of their three closest neighbors.

• Complete at least two passes through Española behind a lowrider on a Sunday afternoon.

• Be able to say the name Concha Ortiz y Pino de Kleven forwards and backwards without drawing a breath.

• Be able to distinguish "chile" from "chili," a roadrunner from a magpie, *yerba buena* from *oshá*, a steer from a heifer, the Santa Fe Opera from Trader Jack's Flea Market, Tommy Macaione from John Ehrlichman, and a Sikh from a Moslem.

We must, however, reserve the right to deny such special status to those who might represent a "burden to society." This category would be defined as persons who have accepted public assistance during their stay in New Mexico, including stockholders in major corporations that pay no income tax. Such persons would be deported to lower Manhattan.

There are bound to be controversies stirred up by this proposal, yet I believe every objection can be answered.

First and foremost, there are sure to be certain native New Mexicans who will complain that such legislation will discriminate against them, simply because they happen to look like New Yorkers or Texans. That problem can be solved, however, simply by issuing a special ID card imprinted with the word *Nativo*. Any New Mexican suspected of dressing too smartly or talking too quickly would need only to whip out his ID card to prove he was a bona fide *ciudadano*.

There will, no doubt, also be those who will claim they are political refugees, fleeing the far right of Dallas or the far left of Greenwich Village. However, we should not be taken in by that ploy of "political asylum," as the vast majority of these aliens are really economic refugees simply searching for a haven in which to hide their dollars.

It will, of course, fall to New Mexican taxpayers to cough up some of their own hard-earned dollars to finance the enforcement of this new legislation. The apprehension of these crafty illegals will demand a highly skilled immigration police force trained to penetrate and crack the opulent alien rings.

But just think of the sweep our New Mexican *migra* could make during post-opera dinners, film festival parties, and art gallery openings (where some unscrupulous owners have been known to jam as many as one hundred illegals into cramped quarters).

In fact, we might commission, say, an Allan Houser to sculpt a New Mexican version of the Statue of Liberty. It could be a likeness of the Indian leader Popé, holding his knotted cord aloft in one hand and a deerskin in the other, inscribed with the legend: "Give me your affluent, your fashionable, your upwardly mobile masses yearning to stay chic."

That would pack them in. And once they are there, why, we'd bust them.

EDUCATION AND OTHER
LITTLE KNOWN DANGERS

 have a solution to one of the most vexing problems facing New Mexico and, indeed, the nation: the crisis in public education.

Perhaps *crisis* is no longer an adequate word to describe the inadequacy of our public education system that, in spite of increasing rhetoric and resources, continues to earn failing grades.

Ironically enough, the key to my solution to this crisis costs no more than a quarter, the price of a newspaper carrying an Associated Press report of a decision by the Texas State Board of Education. That decision was the latest round fired in a showdown between so-called evolutionists and creationists. The question is whether the evolutionary theories of Charles Darwin should be taught in the Texas public schools.

For many creationists, the question of the origin of man is not an issue of idle scientific speculation. It's the Garden of Eden versus *The Planet of the Apes*, and some of these folks get downright apoplectic when it comes to teaching their sons and daughters about their simian relatives, no matter how far removed they might be.

When you consider that the state of Texas is one of the largest purchasers of textbooks in the nation, and that not even Harcourt Brace Jovanovich, Publishers can afford to publish two different sets of textbooks, you come to understand why the publishing moguls listen when the Lone Star State talks.

In truth, we should all pay attention, for the Texas State Board of Education just may have come up with that elusive solution I was speaking of—the surefire cure for our insidious educational ills. Their resolution of the Darwin vs. *Dios* shootout provides the key. By a vote of twenty-one to three, the board decided that biology textbooks in the state need not mention Darwin's theory of evolution. If you're not going to credit the Creator, well, then, you don't have to talk about Charlie either.

I suggest we implement this startling new educational model on a national level, expunging all doubtful material from our curricula, thereby significantly cutting the cost of education. Savings in the cost of materials alone would be dramatic, since expurgated textbooks would be considerably cheaper to publish and to purchase. Physics texts, for instance, could be condensed by leaving out Einstein; after all, his theories are only of relative importance. Galileo, likewise, could be liquidated, along with Copernicus, since texts have long refused to grant equal time to Ptolemy.

As Lubbock board member James H. Whiteside put it, "Who's to decide who the major innovators are?" Voting with the majority against a compromise proposal that would have included Darwin in a list of the great biologists, Whiteside and his colleagues determined that such a grouping would represent no more than a "difference of opinion."

Though the Texas State Board of Education might find it impossible to distinguish between "major innovators" in the course of human affairs, I certainly can recognize innovative thinking when I see it. If we adapt this philosophy to the curricula, we could streamline our course offerings. In U.S. history classes, for example, we could forego the study of the presidents, as it's only a matter of opinion that Lincoln was a more important president than Calvin Coolidge.

Some courses could be eliminated altogether. Literature, for instance, could go; after all, there are plenty of stories for everybody in the Bible. At any rate, the plays of such notorious humanists as Shakespeare contain, as we all know, dangerous references to devil worship (not to mention the fact that they sometimes even portray members of religious and racial minorities as protagonists).

Similarly, the study of art could be scrapped, thereby guaranteeing that our students would no longer be subjected to the lewd paintings of such voyeurs as Rubens or those naked statues sculpted by the Greeks. Bilingual programs and language study could, likewise, be dispensed with, for if God had intended us to be bilingual, we would have been born speaking two languages.

All of this adds up to significant savings in books and materials, yet more important still would be the money we would save on teachers. Since there would be considerably less material to cover, prospective teachers would require far less education themselves, thereby cutting their own costs and justifying an equivalent lowering of their salaries. Moreover, teachers would undoubtedly have fewer exams to grade and less work to do; in fact, the school year might be shortened, rather than lengthened.

Obviously, the elitist standards we currently impose on our educators could be relaxed under the new system. A wider range of individuals could qualify to become teachers, and local school boards across the nation could draw new applicants from the ranks of the desperately unemployed.

The economic shot in the arm resulting from this educational reform plan represents only the short-term benefits; the long-term effects would be even more dramatic. Once they are freed from the disturbing influence of divergent ideas, our youth would be more content and far less likely to rebel. Dissent would gradually disappear in our society, and people would go back to being happy knowing what their parents knew.

Those Texans know the old adage is true: A little knowledge is a dangerous thing. Better to have none at all.

ONE PERCENT
FOR ETIQUETTE

opping up the final drop of red chile with a crusty chunk of *horno*-baked bread, the father of a family of tourists rose from the feast day table. He approached the Indian woman ladling *chicos* and beans into a huge *olla* on the stove and asked, "How much do we owe you?"

In another part of the pueblo, a white-haired man stirred in bed and opened his eyes to see a young couple, who had wandered into his home, staring back at him as if he were an artifact in a museum exhibit.

As the dancers climbed the steps leading to the kiva entrance, the last man in line turned to chase away a woman with a straw hat and a Nikon following on his heels.

It is just such rude gaffes as these that motivate the Maxwell Museum of Anthropology at the University of New Mexico to sponsor public workshops on "Pueblo Feast Day Etiquette."

Yet, it is not solely the Pueblo Indians who must weather the impoliteness of visitors to this land, which for centuries has been hospitable almost to a fault.

New Mexicans of all cultures and creeds could narrate their own tales about the discourteous behavior of some of our guests. By and large, these travelers are not inherently gauche: it is usually ignorance and culture shock that induce them to ask chamber of commerce volunteers why folks around these mountains live in "mud huts."

What tourists and visitors to New Mexico could use is a healthy dose of simple etiquette, which is why I propose the adoption of the "One Percent for Etiquette" training program.

Funded by one percent of all state tax revenues, the program would be a statewide expansion of the Maxwell Museum model. Under its auspices, special Ports of Etiquette would be established along all major highways entering our state, as well as at the airports. All newcomers to the state would be required to stop at one of the Ports of Etiquette, where they would undergo an initial customs check for such contraband as national magazine articles on the mystique of Santa Fe.

Thereafter, the newcomers would receive courtesy training from a certified Land of Enchantment Etiquette Officer. The intensive workshop would cover a broad spectrum of proper behavioral modes delineated by a task force of decorum experts at the State Office of Etiquette Development. Upon completion of the workshop, all visitors would take the Minimal Etiquette Requirement Exam (MERE). Those passing the exam with a score of seventy-five percent or better would receive an official NICE button, featuring a yellow smiling face with a Zia symbol for a nose, and the legend: "Newcomer Is Courteous Enough."

This proof of successful behavior modification would allow any sufficiently courteous newcomer to travel freely throughout the state and intermingle with our peoples. Naturally, those failing the MERE would be turned away at our borders, though Etiquette Officers would be authorized to issue Etiquette Learning Permits to those individuals they consider to be *nearly* nice enough. Such "students," of course, would be allowed to travel through New Mexico only when accompanied by a certified NICE person.

New Mexicans could expect to reap a handsome return on their one-percent investment in etiquette. For instance, the "Real Estate Purchasing Etiquette" segment of the training regimen would instruct prospective investors and property buyers that the old Spanish maxim *"Mi casa es su casa"* is not intended to be taken literally.

Restaurant owners would be relieved to learn that they would no longer have to explain the difference between red and green chile or the reason why there are no bagels or croissants on their menus, thanks to the "Restaurant Etiquette" component of the program.

We would all benefit from the "New Mexico Driving Etiquette" portion of the program, which would train out-of-state drivers to yield the right-of-way to all sheep, goats, pigs, horses, cattle, chickens, ducks, geese, tractors, octogenarians, and, of course, lowriders. Further, owners of Winnebagos and Airstreams would be conditioned to drive on mountain roads solely between the hours of one o'clock and five o'clock in the morning.

The "Cultural Consciousness Etiquette" segment would make visitors less callous about ethnic traditions. Indian artisans on the Santa Fe Plaza, for example, would no longer be asked if they left their bows and arrows at home in their tepees. Nor would ninth-generation Hispanics have to explain to incredulous tourists that, yes, they really *were* born in Mora or Gallina, and that, no, what they speak is not a foreign language.

Another vital element of the training process would be "Pronunciation Etiquette." Though it would be unrealistic to expect the names Cuyamungue or Nageezi to roll like silk off the visitor's tongue, at least we can hope that Ratón won't rhyme with satin. Business people, from motel owners to service station attendants, could be helpful in reinforcing pronunciation etiquette by requiring their customers to correctly pronounce the names of the local mayor, sheriff, and school board president. Those caught slaughtering the pronunciation of the names would be subject to a "monolingual surtax" tacked onto the cost of any goods or services provided to them.

Repeat offenders would have to be dealt with more severely. Upon the commission of a third mispronunciation, such individuals would have a frown superimposed on the smiling face of their NICE buttons. A further mispronunciation would result in the seizure of the visitor's button and his immediate deportation to the English-Only Containment Facility in Carlsbad.

However, the main thrust of the "One Percent for Etiquette" program should remain positive and constructive. Polite behavior could be advanced by instituting an annual cash award for the most perfectly behaved newcomer to New Mexico. We might call it the Popé Politeness Prize, in memory of the etiquette lesson the famed Indian leader taught the Spaniards three hundred years ago.

All New Mexicans could become involved by sending in their nominations for the award. Nominating ballots would provide for the profiling of each candidate on all etiquette fronts, including the aforementioned categories and such others as: "Moviemaking Etiquette," "Miracle Observing Etiquette," and "Penitente Discussing Etiquette."

After four centuries of invasions that have brought three different flags, New Mexico continues to welcome newcomers with tolerance and grace. The "One Percent for Etiquette" program will help ensure that visitors don't at last wear out that welcome.

IV ◆

EL HOMEBOY
The Personal Voice

LOWDOWN LAUGHS
The Española Joke

o who discovered Española anyway?

Why, Marco Cholo, of course.

You don't have to be a student of southwestern history to know that. But to discover where the Española joke came from—now that's a lowrider of a different color. Yet—*¡qué sanamagón!*—that's exactly what I've been trying to do.

It's no piece of *queque*, this epistemological beat, but somebody's got to tackle the business of determining the origin of unusual cultural phenomena. So I hit the Big Rock Shopping Center in Española and began to investigate. I left no stone unturned— no hubcap untouched—in my relentless pursuit of the real story behind the Española joke.

Forcing a smile was no easy task after hearing for the four hundredth time that lowriders use those tiny steering wheels so they can drive with handcuffs on. Yet, smile I did as I chased down lead after lead.

Ultimately, I had to discard as inadequate, faulty, or downright fallacious numerous theories that initially seemed promising. For instance, a coterie of local altar boys confided in me one Sunday after the 12:30 Mass that they knew who had started the Española joke. They claimed to have evidence that Father Guido Sarducci, former gossip columnist for the Vatican on television's "Saturday Night Live," had turned up in Santa Cruz, New Mexico, posing as a priest at Holy Cross Church. The altar boys suggested that Pope John Paul II, grievously disturbed over the universal dissemination of the Polack joke, had hired Sarducci to impersonate a priest and develop the Española joke in the hopes that it might relieve ethnic pressure on the Poles.

Upon investigation, however, I discovered the entire story was a rather transparent fabrication. None of the Santa Cruz priests, I found, has an Italian accent. Nor do any of them smoke, a habit Sarducci has had for years.

Disappointing as that dead end was, it did suggest another investigative avenue. I seemed to recall my friend and folk humor expert Dr. José R. Reyna once mentioning the Polack joke in the Southwest. I rushed to my bookshelf, pulled down my copy of Reyna's book, *Raza Humor: The Chicano Joke Tradition in Texas*, and, yes, there it was on page twenty-one: "Polack jokes are told by Anglos in Texas as they are in the rest of the country, but the Texas Aggie (Texas A & M University student) has emerged as a numbskull figure, and this cycle has become at least as popular as the Polack joke in Texas."

I slapped the book shut. Of course! Motive was, once again, painfully obvious in my mind. The Texas Aggies had started the Española joke fad, wishing, like the Poles, to de-butt themselves from this skull-numbing cycle of jokes. Only one piece was missing from the puzzle: How did they get the Española jokes across state lines without being detected?

I found it difficult to believe the suggestion made by an acquaintance from Tierra Amarilla. According to his theory, the Aggies somehow had infested their livestock with the jokes. The longhorns had then been shipped to New Mexico, where they transmitted the jokes by means of the highly contagious hoof-in-mouth disease. I discounted that theory because the Río Arriba County agent's office reported that Texas longhorns only rarely have been known to learn new jokes.

I had nearly despaired of getting to the bottom of this Española joke business when fate intervened and abruptly unraveled the mystery. As I chamoised my Dodge Ram one afternoon at the car wash across the river, I overheard an interesting conversation among a group gathered around a midnight-blue Trans-Am. One young man advised a companion about the time and place of the "payoff for this week's cruising."

My curiosity was instantly aroused as I scratched down the

address and time of the meeting. And, lo and behold, the following morning I found a furtive-looking group at the Española Post Office, huddled around the mailboxes. This was the central committee of something called EJE.

At first, I made like my key was stuck in a nearby mailbox. Then I nonchalantly inched closer to the group, pretending to read the latest flyer from Furrow. But once I realized the young men seemed oblivious to my presence, I simply stood behind the apparent leader and surreptitiously scratched down notes.

This was the beginning. Since then I've infiltrated the organization and have been able to piece together the following history. EJE is an acronym for the Española Joke Establishment, a top secret organization of Española citizens from all walks of life. The group was organized a few years ago when several Española natives and longtime residents of the valley met secretly to discuss the population boom in the area and the social, economic, and cultural changes that growth might portend.

In those early meetings, residents expressed the fear that the Española valley was in mortal danger of becoming "Santa-fetized." Others spoke with alarm about the threat of contracting a case of "Taositis." In essence, all were in general agreement. Poor Española, landlocked as she was between chic Santa Fe and artsy Taos, seemed doomed to receive the runoff from the overswollen pair of communities. The traditional, rural quality of life in Española was up on the block.

Sikhs were already to the south. Moslems had moved in to the north. The hills were full of ex-hippies turned solar business accountants. And the Maharishi's advance men were meditating on a transcendent locale for their international levitation center somewhere in these crumbling mesas and apple-sweet *vallecitos*.

The time was ripe for drastic action. EJE conceived of a brilliant idea: They would create a series of awful, self-deprecating jokes that would tarnish Española's image for outsiders, thereby assuring that none of them would move in and wreck the area's tranquility. And so EJE introduced the famous joke about the tornado that touched down in Española and did three million dollars worth of improvements.

EJE's founding fathers were proud of that joke; in fact, it became a slogan for the group, immortalized on buttons and widely used as a secret greeting between EJE members.

"Three million dollars," members would say when answering their phones. If the person on the other end of the line replied, "worth of improvements," the caller knew he was talking to *familia*.

Unfortunately, a radical fringe group developed within the ranks of EJE. This contingent, known as the Don Juan de Oñate Liberation Front, has been responsible for the hard-core Española jokes. Primarily young and college educated, these Oñatistas, as they call themselves, have been influenced by Marx Brothers' movies and the sardonic writings of the late Beatle John Lennon. Little is sacred to these Lennon-Marxists, not even the Española prom queen. Yet, the Oñatistas claim that the old jokes are too timid and conventional to truly scare outsiders off.

Only time will tell whether they are right, but one thing is certain: The Española Joke Establishment has been successful. The organization has spread jokes far and wide. A friend said he was visiting the East not long ago when somebody asked him: "Do you know why they removed all the drive-in windows in Española? Because they were too high."

Of course, rumors abound that Española jokes are losing their punch. Moreover, leaks within the organization's hierarchy (of which this exposé is no doubt the most critical) have plagued EJE. Several unsympathetic groups have caught wind of the ulterior motives of EJE and have pledged to arrest the further spread of the jokes.

Still, EJE officials are not alarmed for, even if the jokes lose their currency, EJE always will have the lowriders. The payoffs, you see, go to the local lowriders, who spend their weekends scouting for out-of-town license plates. As soon as the lowriders spot such a vehicle, they pull up side by side and escort the car in a five mile per hour procession from one end of town to the other.

So, friend, as your ulcers smolder while you are way back in the pack, just remember: This Española joke's on you.

THE BLACKOUT OF '84

ncianos talk about the Frost of '48, the Flood of '32, and the Flu of '18. Before I get much older myself, I'd like to add a new disaster to that list: the Blackout of '84. However, unlike all those previous calamities, the Blackout of '84 was no tragic affair. In fact, the loss of electrical power in the very year George Orwell prognosticated that our collective goose would be cooked ended up being a dark blessing in disguise. As an old *dicho* declares: "*No hay mal que por bien no venga*—There is nothing bad that doesn't result in some good."

It had been snowing the kind of snow guaranteed to create a white Christmas when a faulty transformer at the Hernández substation cut the power for nineteen hours in north-central New Mexico from La Mesilla all the way up to Lumberton.

Now, I'm not about to claim there is anything fun about such a protracted power outage. It wasn't simply that there was no electricity to run the Cuisinart; many of us in the rural north who have our own wells—powered, of course, by electrical pumps—found out just how many times one has to refill the pot on the old wood cookstove with snow in order to melt down enough water to fill a coffeepot. Of course, one first had to dig the old campfire blackened *cafetera* out from under the camping gear stashed on an obscure shelf in the garage because not even Joe DiMaggio himself could get a powerless Mr. Coffee to drip.

And, speaking of camping out, those unfortunate *norteños* who live in all-electric homes with no wood, butane, or kerosene backup heaters found themselves, by nightfall, abandoning their icebox houses to unroll sleeping bags on a neighbor's or relative's living room floor.

One of the major annoyances of the outage, however, had nothing to do with the lack of energy—it was, rather, the lack of information about the situation that was particularly vexing to those of us left in the dark. Without speculating about why such an outage affecting such a large number of people over such an extended geographic area hardly raised a media eyebrow in newsrooms to the south, suffice it to say we *norteños* are used to fighting our battles in isolation.

No doubt one of the reasons so little was reported about the blackout was because there was so little to report. Had such an outage occurred in Santa Fe or, worse yet, Albuquerque, the urbanized masses would have had a far more difficult time coping with powerlessness. After all, we *norteños*, for all our microwaves and satellite dishes, are several paces closer to self-sufficiency than the majority of our more metropolitan neighbors. We still realize that firewood comes from a forest and not a classified ad, and we know which end of the hoe cultivates our chile plants.

Doña Agueda Martínez up in Medanales, for instance, with her hand-drawn well, her outdoor plumbing, and her wood cookstove, probably barely noticed the electricity was off.

Yet, even in the north the prolonged outage offered a glimpse of what a real disaster might be like. Cars and trucks queued up at the only service station in town still pumping gas. A crowd huddled under the portal at Furr's, waiting to be escorted into the generator-lit supermarket for an opportunity to purchase a box of candles and a loaf of bread.

But I began with the observation that the Blackout of '84 actually turned out to be an illuminating experience. It was something like "dancing lessons from God," as novelist Kurt Vonnegut puts it, describing those trying circumstances that end up teaching us something important about our lives. The Blackout of '84 provided just such a "dancing lesson." It was one of those lessons we already know, yet continually fail to practice—namely, the value of talking to one another.

With no power to fire up the TV, the VCR, or the PC, entire families found themselves with nothing else to do but entertain each other. At dinner that evening everyone sat around the table, talking quietly in the soft glow of candles and dusty kerosene lamps.

There was a special beauty about that evening, and it wasn't simply reflected in the way the natural light illuminated the faces around the table. After all, you can throw a romantic candlelight dinner any night of the week, but you know that after the Sara Lee and decaf the dishwasher is only the flick of a switch away.

The essence of this beauty came in the realization that we seem to come together naturally to cope with our mutual problems. It was the understanding that our creature comforts are plugged into technological outlets, but our real power is generated by one another.

After dinner, I strolled outside in the crisp air of west side Española, drinking in the palpable silence that even the neighborhood dogs seemed to be respecting, seeing the streets and *callejones* in a new, snow-reflected moonlight—the tin-roofed adobes painted on a midnight-blue canvas, the surreal tails of piñon smoke etched into a star-pocked sky.

There was a warm glow in every window, and I found myself wondering what was going on behind those windows. How many guitars were being tuned up and played for the first time in years? How many decks of playing cards were being dusted off and shuffled by the fireplace?

How many children and grandchildren were, at that moment, hearing the names of relatives they never knew they had and family stories they could never have imagined?

How many of these homes were being visited by *la Llorona,* that lady of sorrow so out of fashion these days, banished into blinding obscurity by the light bulb?

How many *ancianos* who sit mutely before a television set night after night were now telling the old stories, the wonderful *cuentos* of *la vida de antes,* life back in the old days when things really *were* rough? That foot of snow outside—*pues, no es nada.* Back then, they had biblical weather—snow so deep it peaked above the horses' haunches, cold so bitter that cattle froze on all fours, keeling over dead in the spring thaw.

It's those stories, told across the table and passed down through the generations, that keep the culture of New Mexico alive; yet, we never seem to think of telling them when the lights are on. Perhaps we ought to cut the juice at least once a week, strike a match to the kerosene lamp, and simply listen to the stories unfolding in the darkness.

We just might find ourselves there.

TALKING RONALD REAGAN
One Writer's "Muse Blues"

onald Reagan woke up to find himself transformed into Beetle Bailey," he wrote.

He scrutinized the single line sprawled on the blank page like a *lombriz kafkaiana*, puffed on his *bahiano hediondo,* and suddenly scratched the whole thing out. It was his fifth false start in two hours, and it was worse than ever.

Quería comentar sobre la crisis en Centroamérica. He wanted, somehow, to spill his anger out over the page. He was thinking in terms of messages—*estaba pensando mal otra vez.*

It was something like the poem he had written the day before:

> *Hay tantas casas blancas*
> *en los Estados Unidos*
> *y en cada una*
> *hay un portal*
> *donde un joven pálido*
> *toma una coke y juega*
> *con una carabina*
>
> *En la mira está el indio*
> *la gente de color*
> *el mundo*

He had liked it well enough at first, but then he realized it didn't do anything—*no tenía chispa*. When would he ever learn not to work from a theme?

What he needed—*malamente*—was a visit from his *tía* Beatriz. She hadn't been around for weeks. *She'd* know what to do. *Bueno, él también sabía lo que diría ella*, but he had to hear *her* say it because. . . *pues*, because she was his muse.

Más anciana que los álamos en la acequia, tía Beatriz was, at the same time, too young to ignore a single sunrise. She was male as well as female, as much at home hopping a gold-flecked, T-topped, diamond-tucked '67 lowride Impala as she was hitching up the mares in the *bogue* to go to a neighbor's *velorio*.

She was strong—*eso sí*—always able to take care of herself. When she was younger she could lift the anvil with one hand, and she's always built her own house. *Era muy sharpe también*—she learned mechanics, carpentry, and plumbing because she never believed in *pagando a alguien dioquis* when she could do the job herself. And when her *perrita* would go into heat, *pues nomás le ponía panties*—one of her old pairs, and the bitch would never have a litter.

Era loca la tía Beatriz—no question about that. Once, she gave herself a home permanent and left the harsh chemicals on over-night because she figured she'd end up with tighter *rizos*, but in the morning her hair came off with the rollers, *y ella se quedó medio pelada*.

She lived for her *huerta*—her garden, her chickens, her goats, and her milk cow. She loved music too—always had her radio *puesta*, tortuously loud, *y siempre en la misma estación*: KBSO (*¡Que beso!*). *Le encantaban Tiny Morrie y Baby Gaby*, just as she loved Victor Jara and Silvio Rodríguez. *También le cuadraba el boxing*—and that *lucha libre* that came out on Sunday mornings when she came home from mass. She always rooted for Ricky Romero even though she knew it was all a big show—*en efecto, todo lo que salía en el mono era una bola de mentiras*. Like that *barullo* about men landing on the moon—*pues, todo el mundo sabía que era un engaño*, a government show secretly staged in the desert.

Y las telenovelas—¡*válgame Dios!*—the cast of the "Days of Our Lives" *era como su propia familia*, and *tía* Beatriz would discuss their daily tragedies at the dinner table right along with her *compadre's* cancer and his *bisnieta's primera comunión*.

She had a memory that stretched back to the long years of sheepherding in Utah and the racist womb of the Colorado silver mines. She even remembered her great-great-grandfather, *el primer poblador del pueblo*, who slashed an *entrada* into the wilderness with his team of *bueyes*.

The single frustration of her life was that she never got to be a nun. But, like any *monja*, *tía* Beatriz had a secret fascination with sex and would hover over his shoulder while he penned a good scene, more often than not suggesting one of her *chistes cochinos*.

Like that joke about her *comadre*. *Izque la tía Beatriz* was on her way to a dance in a horse and buggy with her *comadre* and her husband. All of a sudden the horses got spooked, and the buggy flipped on its side, throwing the three of them in the ditch. "*¿Estás bien, compadre?*" *tía* Beatriz asked her *comadre's* husband, who was lying beside her in the *acequia*. When he didn't answer *tía* Beatriz, she started feeling for him in the darkness. What she didn't know was that her *compadre* had torn his pants in the fall. *De repente, tía* Beatriz shouted to her *comadre*: "*¡Ay comadre—ya mi compadre se destripó!*"

Tía Beatriz never became a nun because both of her parents perished in the Great Influenza of 1918, leaving her to take care of her nine younger brothers and sisters. Her mother was half Indian *por el lado de su papá* who had been a Navajo slave, but now *tía* Beatriz's own *hijas* were married to *gabachos* who did weapons research in Los Alamos, *y sus nietos ya ni sabían hablar con ella en español*.

Which was probably why she liked to talk so much, and he took full advantage of it, writing down her memories *y sus mil modos de hablar* that included everything from the antiquated *español de Cervantes* to the *caló de los pachucos*. And she always told him—if you've *gotta* write it, *pos píntalo lo mesmo como lo digo*.

Pero algunas veces él se agüitaba, and he'd complain that if he wrote it all *revuelto asina*, neither the *gringo* publishers nor the *latinoamericanos* would touch his work, and he didn't need the fingers of even one hand to add up all the bilingual publishing houses.

"*¿Qué te importa, siendo nuestro modo de hablar?*" *respondía la tía Beatriz*, always urging him to work from reality. Not that he had to write like a tape recorder, but the characters that flowed from his *pluma* had to be believable—*carne y hueso*, not prancing ghosts.

And this dilemma of how to write about Reagan, this anger that cried out for a plot—well, he knew exactly what *tía* Beatriz would tell him. She'd say—sure, write it, just as she had told him to write about Primo Ferminio, the political *patrón* who had controlled the county for more than three decades by hook *and* crook. *Claro que sí—escribe de la política*, but use everything you know, and make sure the black hats have a feather or two *y los sombreros blancos algunas manchitas*.

And he laughed, for he realized *tía* Beatriz had been there all along. And now he simply picked up his pen and listened.

"¿Sabes por qué la gente de Nuevo México votó por Reagan?" tía Beatriz asked him. *"Pos, cuando andaban en misa, oían al padre decir—'ruega por nosotros.'* Υ *los pobres nuevomexicanos pensaban que decía, 'Reagan por nosotros.'* Since the priest himself was telling them to vote for that old *sanamabitche, pus* they all went out and did it."

La tía Beatriz se rió y dijo, "I don't know how you can use that joke in your story, but I'm sure you'll find a way."

And she went outside to split some firewood.

"LA ESPAÑOLA"

 o some, she's the hydraulic-hopping, slow and *suave* lowrider capital of the United States.

To others, she's the butt of a seemingly endless cycle of inane jokes.

But to those of us who call Española, New Mexico, our home, she is the enigmatic "Spanish lady" her name implies.

She may be dressed during business hours in her Lotaburger uniform, but beneath that cap and hair net are the dark locks of a thousand years of history braiding the great cultures of the Río Grande valley into a single, unbroken strand.

You just need to meet her after she gets off work and lets her hair down. You'll have to look for her, not in the parking lot at the Big Rock Shopping Center, but in the places she lives—in the mud-plastered adobe home her great-grandfather built in the healing shadow of the Santuario de Chimayó—at her hand-hewn *telar* in Medanales, where she weaves her *frezadas de garras,* the mottled rag rugs that endure the red dust tracked in by generations of work shoes—in her living room with its textured walls literally covered with school photos, ancestral wedding pictures, and full-color portraits of sad-eyed grandsons in marine uniforms next to the Sacred Heart of Jesus and the last couple of popes, the place where she spends her evenings sitting in front of a television set she never watches while she shapes snakey clay coils into the thin walls of a pot later to be fired under horse dung in the center of the world at Santa Clara Pueblo.

To know "la Española," you've got to find out where she lives.

That, of course, is the hard part, for she lives off the beaten track in this town that grew up around the railroad tracks of the Chili Line that once transported the wool and bright chile *ristras* of this fertile *valle* to eastern markets.

Though those tracks have long since disappeared beneath the asphalt memory of the original commercial center where Peoples, née Bond and Williards, once stood, the Anglo-mercantile-entrepreneurial era is recent history in this most ancient of places.

If you want to know the real face of "la Española," you'll have to venture off the main drag and follow the great river north just like Juan de Oñate did nearly four centuries ago when he set up the first European capital in the Southwest across the river from the Pueblo site of Yunge Oweenge, which he promptly rechristened "San Juan de los Caballeros." Though the new name stuck, the Tewas never lost their older identity, the one written in the volcanic rocks over the river and in the primordial beat of the drum that "la Española" dances to, a dream, a vision, butterfly, and cloud.

You'll find her dancing, too, at the Casa Nova Nightclub in Alcalde, her face shining as she ducks under the pulsating human bridge of *la marcha*, the traditional "Wedding March" being played through overloaded amplifiers by the *nietos* and *bisnietos* of elderly *músicos* who once fiddled and strummed the old *piezas,* the wonderfully ritualized *valses, cuadrillas*, and *varsovianas*— "put your little foot right there."

It may take some footwork to find this elusive lady, a little climbing, perhaps, to reach her high on the cliffs of Puyé, where she gazes out of a cave blackened by the fires of her indigenous ancestors. But, as you follow her eyes that trace the flight of the hawk gliding on the hot air currents below you in the impossibly turquoise sky, you'll know the climb was worth it.

Afterwards, you can find her in the funky tepee booth at Angelina's Restaurant, talking politics and swapping family stories over steamy *sopaipillas* and long-necked Buds, her eyes dancing with laughter that suddenly erupts in rolling waves of *gusto*, the pure joy of doing all the simple things of life without worrying who's looking.

If you join her at that lamplit table, however, be prepared to put your watch away along with your *ansias*, for "la Española" is never in a hurry to finish anything, especially a warm and juicy *conversación*. Don't be in a rush to know her either, for, in spite of her alluring smile, she's a remarkably private lady, a personality trait acquired over centuries of isolation in this northern frontier where she has had to tolerate successive waves of invaders from Franciscan friars to Hog Farm freaks.

Still, you will find her gracious and inviting, for hospitality is at the center of her multicultural tradition. "*Mi casa es su casa*," she continues to say, even today, even after so many have taken her literally and forced her out of her house, her *rancho*, her *ejidos*, her forests, and her farmlands, reducing her to a five-hundred-square-foot plot in a trailer court.

You're more than welcome to come into that trailer home—"*Pase, siéntese*"— but you must remember to be respectful. For, "la Española" is as proud as she is intriguing, and if you can't see the eagle in her black eyes—if you are deaf to the flowing cadences of her Spanish tongue—if you refuse to respect her wisdom and hard-won faith, she will turn her beautiful back on you and go on her mysterious way, leaving you to dig in your bag of cold french fries at the Stop and Eat drive-in.

PORTRAITS

LIBERATO MONTOYA

agpies chatter raucously in the nearby *bosque* where the Chama River flows into the Río Grande. The Tewas have been here since their Anasazi ancestors settled in this fertile river valley, and Liberato Montoya looks as if he has been sitting under this cottonwood nearly that long. His rawhide hands clutch a cane mended with black electrician's tape, a cane planted as firmly as the Spanish flag don Juan de Oñate drove into this very ground nearly four centuries ago. Spitting into that historical dust near the feet of a mangy pueblo dog, Mano Liberato—as he is universally known in the valley—cracks a *chifonete* grin and announces:

"I'm just a ninety-year-old kid, but I like to dance anyway."

Of course, enjoyment is one thing, but survival is a far more important issue, and you should know immediately that Mano Liberato dances strictly for money.

"I've gotta pay my light bill—I'm not gonna dance for *nothin'*," he says, which is why he rises at dawn and hitchhikes the twenty-five miles to the capital, inching down the highway with his back in a permanent forty-five-degree stoop and lugging a dusty suitcase bound with frayed clothesline cord. Once he has arrived at the Palace of the Governors and "hustled some tourists," as he puts it, Mano Liberato pulls his full Indian costume from the valise—the thread-bare paisley shirt, stabilized-turquoise necklace, bells, and hundred-dollar feather headdress. Then he'll proceed to dance—after negotiating his fee, of course.

Yes, it'll cost you a few bucks, but it will be the most unique Indian dance you'll ever see, as the sway-backed elder leaps, grinds, and gyrates in a style more reminiscent of John Travolta than the Buffalo Dance. And the music—well, it begins with a chant that sounds Tewa enough to the untrained ear, but soon it screeches headlong into an incomprehensible traffic jam of tone and language. You'll probably have to witness several performances before you realize Mano Liberato is actually singing a double-time chorus of: "The old grey mare she ain't what she used to be."

Mano Liberato's old bones ain't what they used to be anymore either, but he's hardly ready to *colgar los tenis*. In fact, in the last decade since his wife "passed out"—the *viejo's* original euphemism for dying—he's belonged to one of those mail-order bride clubs. "I pay twenty bucks for the club, and women from all over the world write to me. They all wanna marry me—they all want my money. They tell me, I can't find another man *like* you. Now, a twenty-three-year-old lady, this lady from Texas, she wanna come and *marry* me."

Though it's anyone's guess whether Mano Liberato really will tie the knot with his mercenary *novia,* there's no doubt his memory is as deeply rooted as those *alamos* down by the river that once formed the boundary between the first Spanish capital of New Mexico and the ancient pueblo of Yunge Oweenge at the turn of the sixteenth century. And somehow it's fitting that this tricultural patriarch who speaks Tewa, Spanish, and English, and who is as much at home in the lobby of La Fonda Hotel as he is in the womb of the kiva, should live atop the ruins of San Gabriel, the site where the two traditional cultures of New Mexico first intermingled. In fact, Mano Liberato's own upbringing was a result of that long-standing tradition of cultural exchange: born of Hispanic parents, as a young boy he was adopted and raised by an Indian family at San Juan Pueblo.

But Mano Liberato tells the story much better himself, and, like the storytellers of the past, he begins at the very beginning. "My daddy came from *way* back in *them* years. In them days, there was a lota deer—I mean, a lota buffalo then. My grandpa, he was a *rich* guy. He had five thousand sheep and gold—he was a pretty rich guy, I guess. And in them days he used to say, from that peak there in Trinidad—over in Colorado—on over to Walsenburg—that land's all mine. Anyway, he used to say that country was all *his*, so that's how he got rich, and my daddy—he's movin' over here to San Juan, and there was *no* store, no *nothin'*, so my daddy went and put up a store and a saloon, and there was some gamblin' and he made all *kinds* of money. And then he got stuck on my mother, and she was only ten years old. He said, I wanna marry you *darlin'*, and she had eighteen kids—boys and girls. Eighteen kids—that's what she had—they used to marry 'em young in them days.

"I was born in 1891. I was born down there under a tree, the way I understand it. So lightning came up and—I don't know how true it *is*—but the story is that some lightning came and, I don't know, picked me up and *threw* me in the garden—in the chile over there."

Tangling with lightning, however, was nothing compared to dealing with those nuns in grade school. "It was in 1904— no, in 1902—let's see, how old was I?—in 1902—no, 1903— 1903?—no, in 1904, and they sent me to school in St. Catherine's, but I didn't *like* it there. The *monjas* were too mean—beat the *shit* outa you all the time. They used to pull my ears like that," he says, demonstrating the sisters' technique on his rather awesome set of ears.

School, clearly, was not for Mano Liberato, so when a labor contractor from Chimayó showed up at St. Catherine's looking for young men willing to work in the beet fields of Rockyford and La Junta, Colorado, the lightning-struck boy was ready to go. But his father, apparently, had other ideas.

"I told my daddy I'm gonna go up to *Colorado* and *work*. And he says *no*—you are too *young*—they're not going to pay you. You're gonna work *here*, and he says you gotta be here when the sun rises—make sure *be* here—then we won't come back till eight o'clock tonight—pretty dark. You mean to say we're gonna work day and *night?* And my daddy says, well, he says, we need the money and—*twenty-five cents a day?* We're gonna work for twenty-five cents a *day? Shut up!*—my daddy told me—I'm gonna *kill* you! So I said, *mátame*—go ahead and *kill* me, but I'm not gonna work for twenty-five cents a day. I wanna go work over there—in *Colorado*. What's the *matter* with you? *Wham!*—and then—*Wham!* Daddy, I said, don't *do* that to me. No, I'm gonna *kill* you!'"

Mano Liberato illustrates the dialogue with a little spontaneous role-playing, as his long-dead "daddy" delivers several devastating backhand *cachetadas*, each of which the elder "receives" in the classic Hollywood style, at one point nearly losing his balance and tumbling off the weather-stripped table that serves as his seat.

By now the afternoon is waning, and we've still only gotten to 1904—or is it 1903? There are so many more questions to ask—so much more territory to cover. What about New Mexico's transformation from a territory to a state? Does Liberato remember the statehood celebration of 1912?—the 1918 influenza?—World War I and II?—the Great Depression? What can he tell us about Teddy Roosevelt—Tom Catron—the kaiser—Albert Bacon Fall?

"*I'm* tellin' this story now," Mano Liberato snaps, angrily twisting his cane into the ground. "I'm tryin' to tell this story *good*," he says, returning to the monologue of his personal adventures as a child in the early years of this century. And the *anciano* is right where we left him, still battling with his daddy over leaving for Colorado. He does eventually get on a train to Alamosa, apparently without the knowledge of his daddy—or, for that matter, the blessing of his mother.

"Mother, I'm leavin'. Where you going, *malcriado*? I wanna blanket to go to *Colorado*. You're not gonna get *nothin'*. Anyways, I took off—I didn't had no shoes on—I didn't had no money. So we stop at Alamosa—we had to stay there that night. So we sing and dance *all* night long. So anyway, that Spanish guy, he comes the next morning and I ask him—*¿Qué no nos va a dar de almorzar?* But he say we gotta *pay* for our breakfast—*y si no quieren pagar, busquen qué comer*. Well, I got no money, and in *them* times, wheat was only fifty cents a hundred pounds, corn was fifty cents, and sugar was two cents a pound. Coffee a cent and a half a pound, and you could get a whole *sack* for a dollar and a half—I mean fifty pounds of coffee and then you had to grind it—you had to buy a *grinder* and grind it—so in *them* days there was no money—so what are you gonna do *now*?

"So anyways, we stayed there a while and so here comes a hobo, a *trampe* or whatever you call him—and he says, are you hungry? And I say, yeah, I'm pretty hungry. Me, too, he said—but you know what? That lady over there—I went over there and asked her for—to gimme some breakfast, or gimme a piece of bread, and she say for me to chop some wood. I don't have to chop no wood. So I says, let me go. *Oiga señora, ¿cómo le va? ¿Qué anda haciendo aquí?*—she tell me, so I say I'm hungry—*ando muerto de hambre—ando de trampe—quiero comer.* So she give me the *hacha*, and I went and chopped *wood*—a lota wood—and she gave me two piece of bread and some meat—some tortillas. I didn't wanna *starve* so I chopped *wood*."

Even though we never actually arrive at the beet fields of Colorado in the story—the trip, apparently, is of far greater importance than what transpired at the destination—we can be sure of one thing: Mano Liberato never starved up in Colorado, and he has never wanted for much during his ninety years under the New Mexican sun. He's worked hard, and when hard work hasn't been enough, he's relied on his wits, his three languages, and his ability to dance between cultures.

"Now I'm all set," he says. "I'm dancin'—I got my pension. I went to the war—I joined the army in 1915—1915?—no, 1914, it was—1915? My daddy told me I can't go—I said, Daddy, I wanna go—I don't care if they *kill* me—I'm gonna get my *pension*. Then I came back and I got stuck on my wife. When she was twenty-one years old, I came back from the army—in 19 . . . ?—19 . . . ?—and she was *writin'* to me. So when I came back, I say, you are twenty-one—you better *marry* me. So she said, I'm gonna marry you because you went to the army, and I'm gonna get a check when I get *old*. So that's it—I'm gonna marry you because I *like* you and I'm gonna get *money*. These other guys—they can't give me a penny—they're no good for *nothin'*. And you, right here you gave me five *dollars*—so I'm gonna *marry* you for that five dollars.

"So I got married and we had a big feast. I bought her a big steer and *five* goats. We had all that meat, so we invite all the Pueblos—from Taos and Picurís—we had a *big* feast. It cost me four hundred dollars—in *them* days. I brought a lota money from the army—and we made fifty-three years. She pass out in 1971—and now I'm by myself and I do *dancin'*— and I make fifty dollars, one hundred dollars at La Fonda—so you want me to put on the feathers?"

"Putting on the feathers" turns out to be a major undertaking, as the *anciano* painstakingly hobbles past the twin *hornos* and crumbling *choza* into his austere, fortlike adobe. After he finally wedges his arthritic arms into the faded paisley shirt, he pulls on his Indian headdress, but unfortunately he has forgotten to put on his turquoise necklace first, so he must remove the feathers in order to put on the beads, after which he puts the headdress on backwards—

but, at last the costume is in place. "Before, I look like a Mexican. This way I look like an Indian—that's where the *money* is," he says.

And, speaking of money, Mano Liberato says, "*Acuérdate que hay un Jesucristo*," —in other words, where's his pay?

"All these pictures you're takin'—you can't fool me. You're makin' *plenty* of money. People pay me thirty-five dollars—forty dollars for my picture. No sir—you can't trick me. A guy over in Santa Fe sold my picture right in front of me for two hundred and fifty bucks, and I only charged him *six*! No sir—*Con noventa años no estoy pendejo*—I gotta have a little money. I gotta pay my *light* bill."

After we settle on a figure that's at least, in Mano Liberato's words, "better than nothin'," the *anciano* announces in his crisp, professional tone: "This is an Indian song from San Juan. I learned that song a *long* time ago—about 1911, I think—and I *couldn't* forget it."

And he leaps into his dance, headdress swaying, bells jingling, and shoulders gyrating. "Old grey mare she ain't what she useta be," he sings, twirling and weaving precariously between the carcasses of the broken-down appliances that litter his yard. But he can't fool us—no sir. Somewhere beneath those rotting refrigerators and stoves are the ruins of the first capital of New Mexico. And underneath that hundred-dollar headdress is a true *nuevomexicano*—a man of three languages and cultures, a shrewd survivor, a "ninety-year-old kid."

A dancer.

SOSTENES TRUJILLO

hort and stout, Sostenes Trujillo greets us with a back-cracking *abrazo,* immediately taking us under her wing. "*Entren, entren hijitos,*" she addresses us like long-lost grandchildren, shepherding us into her warm kitchen. The summery scent of *yerba buena* permeates the bright room, which is appropriate since the seventy-four-year-old woman is an herbalist, one of the best-known *curanderas* in Chimayó.

We've come to learn about the folk medicine she's practiced all her life, and Sostenes has done her homework. "You know, *hijito,* last night I sat down and thought about everything in the past—all the *remedios* I knew. And I couldn't even remember half of them," she says, shaking her head with its frizzy white crown of hair, which looks less like a beauty shop permanent than the even more permanent upshot of her own internal electricity.

"I told her she better not fall asleep because then she wouldn't remember a single one of the *remedios,*" remarks her husband, Juan, his eyes smiling through the opaque *vidrio* of his spectacles.

"*No le hagas nada aprecio,*" returns Sostenes—"Don't pay any attention to him. Just because he's a year older than me, he likes to pick on me all the time."

And they both laugh, Juan with his eyes, and Sostenes—well, she laughs with her entire body, relishing this latest skirmish in their war of words. The ongoing sparring match keeps the pair of *viejitos* alert and on their linguistic toes—it's a thoroughly healthy battle.

And health is what brought us to the door of this *curandera,* who says she learned the art of folk medicine from her mother, Liorera Pacheco, a *médica* in Truchas during the last century. From her earliest days, Sostenes recalls having possessed the gift of healing, and what better evidence of that than the fact that the *curandera* had four of her eight babies entirely by herself. "No one else was there," she says—"not even a *partera* (midwife)."

In the course of raising those eight children, Sostenes prepared countless teas from the *yerbas* she gathered along the nearby hillsides and arroyos, but she also made plenty of plasters and ointments for her *vecinos* in El Ojito, where she lived with her first husband. Unfortunately, no amount of herbs could help her first *esposo*, who ultimately died of cancer. "*El era un gringo,*" she observes. "Then I got married to this *mexicano* here."

Before "this *mexicano*" can fashion a fitting retort to his wife, I do what visitors to Sostenes's home have done for half a century—I hit her up for some free advice. What can I do for this cough I can't seem to shake?

The answer to the question lasts well over an hour, and takes us on a journey from the scalp to the toes. And though we investigate all the major and minor calamities that can befall this all too delicate flesh, the trip is fun, sidetracking constantly into *chistes* and *adivinanzas,* the traditional jokes and riddles of a people who have learned to survive centuries of hardship and disease with self-effacing humor.

"*El que lo compra no lo usa, y él que lo usa no lo mira,*" Sostenes declares at one point, challenging us to figure out the answer to the *adivinanza*—"He who buys it does not use it, and he who uses it never sees it." The answer, of course, is a coffin—*el cajón del difunto.*

But we were involved with less serious matters a moment ago—*esta tos,* this nagging cough. *Poleo,* a variety of mint that grows along the ditches in the area, makes an effective tea, Sostenes indicates. The herb *estafiate* is also good, she adds, "mixed with *miel virgen* (honey) or *piloncillo* (native brown sugar)." And there's also the familiar *limón con miel virgen y juisque,* lemon tea with honey and whiskey. "You just give this tea to the *niños, y se ponen muy tranquilos,*" Sostenes says, pantomiming a child dropping off to sleep.

I've also had a bit of a sour stomach lately, but say no more—Sostenes knows just what works to relieve *ese dolor de la panza.* The herb *altamisa* is powerful, as well as *inmortal, pazote,* and the commercially prepared and ever popular *aceite mexicano. Cota* (Navajo tea) and *yerba buena,* the *curandera* continues, are good for kidney and bladder difficulties. Diarrhea in babies can be cured with lavender (*alhucema*). Earaches are no problem if you have a little *volcánico* or *tabaco hervido.* And if you're a touch squeamish about packing a plug of boiled chewing tobacco into your ear, consider the common *remedio* for extracting foreign objects from the eye—*un frijol.* Yes, you insert a pinto bean under the eyelid and drag it over the surface of the eye. "It sounds funny, but it works," Sostenes says— "*por la gracia de Dios*—through the grace of God."

Throughout our talk, Sostenes repeats a similar phrase: "*Todo está en el poder de Dios*—Everything is in the hands of God. I only help."

For Sostenes, this recognition of God's power is more than a simple belief. It's at the center of the *viejita's* upbringing, and it is a *crianza* anchored in respect. "*Yo me acuerdo que antes de ir al baile, nos hincábamos para la bendición*—I remember before we'd go to a dance, we used to kneel before our parents for their blessing," Sostenes says, recalling a custom that has all but vanished in these mountains. And no one is more aware than Sostenes herself of how much times have changed. "*Es muy diferente ahora*; now, the little ones run around screaming—*pues, ¡gritan como animales!*"

School was different in her day as well, the *curandera* says. "When we were going to school, my mama would pack our lunch. And do you know what it was? An apple and a tortilla with *chicharrones* (pig cracklings). That was it. Now, it's *puros jamborgues* with the kids—all the time, *¡Vamos pa' McDonalds, vamos pa' McDonalds!*"

Sostenes squints, purses her lips, and shrugs her shoulders in a gesture of distaste for "*esas porquerías*"—that junk food she sees as being part of the reason young people are so unhealthy nowadays. "We used to harvest the *alverjón*," she continues, referring to the native peas that are a staple of many of the small *huertas* of the area. "We'd peel them and then sew the *alverjones* together with thread. Once they were dried, we'd store them. Then, when my papa would kill a *becerro,* we'd get some of the bones with a little meat on them, and we'd make a stew with the *alverjón. ¡Tan sabroso!*"

Juan shifts uncomfortably on the bed. "*Ahora que esta mujer está hablando de carne, me está dando hambre,*" he says. The *anciano's* stomach may be growling now that the conversation has turned to the subject of meat, but, as Juan says, the people of the past rarely went hungry. "*Más antes nos ayudábamos, los unos a los otros,*" he says—"In the old days, we all used to help each other out. We didn't know what hunger was back then. If a *vecino* killed a pig, why he'd give you a piece of meat."

Like most of his relatives and neighbors, Juan lived the life of a *ranchero* until the coming of World War II. The end of that war ushered in the demise of much of the subsistence farming in northern New Mexico; like so many of his generation, Juan found himself taking an eight-to-five job in order to survive in the new "money economy."

Though Juan worked for the State Highway Department for many years, he never lost his love for working the land. And now that he's retired, he still tends his garden—"*para divertirme,*" as he puts it—"to entertain myself. And to eat melons. I've got some goats and rabbits now too. I used to have cattle and horses, but not anymore. That's too much work for me now. *No, ahora todo lo que tengo son años*—all I have now are a lot of years."

"But people were stronger in those days, *hijito,*" Sostenes interjects. "Now, people are always at the doctor's office, day and night, and it doesn't even help—*Tras y tras con los doctores, y nada*. Throwing away all that money. Why, if I just give them a good *sobada,* they get better," she says, kneading her powerful fingers on imaginary flesh.

"There was a woman who came by the other day, limping—*venía cojiando, ves*. But I gave her a good massage, and she ended up throwing away her cane. *Sí, ¡tiró la muleta!*"

Sostenes is perhaps best known for her ability as a *sobadora*. "*Día a día viene gente para una sobada*—Day in and day out, people come for a massage," the *viejita* says. The only problem is that she doesn't have a *licencia,* as she puts it.

"*Cuidado—te van a echar en la pinta,*" crows Juan—"Watch out or they'll throw you in the pen."

Of course, even if Sostenes did end up in the *pinta* for working without a license, they probably wouldn't be able to keep her there for long. Suddenly she changes the subject, clapping her hands as she announces: "I *love* to go to parties! We go to the senior citizens. And we're the ones who dance up on the platform. We've even come out in the newspaper and on TV for dancing!"

And if I were scratching away at a violin instead of a steno pad, the sprightly *viejita* would no doubt demonstrate a few *varsovianas* right on the kitchen floor. We settle, instead, for a cup of coffee and continue our conversation between bites of fresh *bizcochitos*.

"You know what I found the other day?" Juan asks as his wife continues *trafiquiando* with the coffeepot. "*Un tecolote*—an owl. It was outside the window on the patio. I thought it was a chicken at first until I saw how big it was. It started to fly away, but I was able to kill it with my *muleta*. I took it out to the garage there and burned it. And you know, the next morning when I went there, I only found a little ash—no bones, nothing—*nomás ceniza*."

"*Era una bruja*," Sostenes shudders, and we begin a round of witch stories, a cultural custom as ageless as the piñon wood that once burned in the fireplaces families huddled around to tell *brujerías*. And the stories still possess their mesmerizing effect. *Bolas de lumbre*—fireballs come bouncing out of nowhere. Demonic dogs, black as the night that spawned them, pursue terrified children through an endless maze of arroyos. And *brujas* work evil curses on their hapless victims with poisonous preserves and deadly posole.

Juan tells the story of a *tío* of his who stopped into a *viejita's* house one afternoon to escape the rain. "*La viejita tenía tortillas en la estufa*—The old lady had some tortillas cooking on the stove. She invited my uncle to sit down and eat. My *tío* said no, that he had to be on his way, but the *viejita* insisted he take a tortilla with him. Well, my *tío* got on his horse and tore open that hot tortilla, *y estaba lleno de gusanos vivos*—it was full of live worms. And he had seen her just take it off the stove!—*¡Del comal lo había sacado!*"

At that instant the screen door rattles, startling us all. "*Es el gato*," Sostenes tells us—it's only Pinkie the cat asking to come in now that it's getting dark. Only then do I notice the time and realize twilight has shrouded the sandy hills of Chimayó. A full moon is already peeking over the jagged Sangre de Cristos, and we must leave. But not without another round of *abrazos*, a sack of yellow apples, and a "*cuídense bien, hijitos*."

Yes, I assure Sostenes, we'll be careful. We'll watch out for *brujas* and bad drivers, for *el empache y el aigre*, and we'll keep away from those *porquerías de jamborgues*. And if we're ever aching for a good *sobada* or just a good cup of coffee and a healing laugh, we know where to find the *curandera*.

MAX TRUJILLO

ne foot pounds a bass drum while the
other slaps a cymbal in rhythmic counter-
point. Now the electric guitar kerplunks
the bright waltzy melody, and he's cooking. The seventy-seven-year-old throws
back his silver-maned head and joyfully bellows an upbeat rendition
of "*Las Mañanitas*" into the overloading microphone: "*Quisiera ser
el solecito pa' entrar por tu ventana, y darte los buenos días acostadita en tu
cama*—I'd like to be the sun so I could come in through your window and wish you a good morning while you're still lying in your
bed."

He's Max Trujillo, Taos's original one-man band, and when he
painted "*Música Fabricada por Max C. Trujillo*" on the front of his
homemade music machine, he really meant it. For he "makes" not
only the music, but all his instruments as well.

"I get 'em from right here," Max grins, pointing meaningfully
to his head. "I just pick 'em up myself. Nobody teach me nothin'. I
make everything since scratch."

And that he does.

The bass drum, for instance, is the copper core of a Salvation
Army washing machine covered with a deerskin. Max, of course,
peeled and cured the *cuero* that resounds with each syncopated beat
of the hinged foot pedal.

The guitar, actually, was the first instrument Max made. Working with a chunk of avocado wood from California, Max fashioned
that first guitar before he knew how to finger a single chord. He's

always done it that way: "First, I make 'em, then I figure out how to play 'em," he says.

And it must have required a considerable amount of "figuring" to learn how to play this unique twelve-string guitar that features four sets of three strings rather than the standard six sets of two. "I betcha Roberto Mondragón couldn't play this one," Max says, referring to the popular folk musician and former lieutenant governor of New Mexico.

Mondragón, no doubt, would have even less luck with another one of Max's original stringed creations, his "reversible mandoharplin." The name is my own; Max has never named the outlandish instrument—it was hard enough to make it! One side of the musical contraption is a handmade mandolin strung in Max's singular style. Turn the instrument over and you've got a dulcimer-like harp operated by lettered keys resurrected from an antique typewriter.

Max plays the instrument like a typewriter, too, pecking out a *varsoviana*: Put your little foot—A-Q-D-Y-D—Put your little foot—right there—SHIFT.

But what else can he play on his keyboard harp? Well, there's that fast one, that English song that rattles along at—well, it must be at least forty-five notes a minute—*pero, ¿cómo se llama?* Max can't recall the name until he starts knocking out the tune: "Oh, '*Isla de Capri*'!" he suddenly remembers.

Of course, you can't fault the self-made *músico* for not remembering the title of every *pieza* in his repertoire because it's as varied as it is extensive, including everything from "You Are My Sunshine" to epic *entriegas de novios,* the long, episodic songs traditionally sung to newlyweds at wedding feasts. Max even composes some of his own tunes, like his *corrido* entitled "*El pobre y el rico*," a rambling ballad based on the classic confrontation between the rich and the poor.

Max, likewise, performs for rich and poor alike, though his major bookings tend to be at the senior citizen centers in and around his hometown of Taos. And Max doesn't need a stage or a PA system—just provide him with an outlet to plug in his amplifier, and he'll truck his rig over to play. It's all one unit: the instruments have their own customized cases built into a plywood platform tied together with the cast-iron remnants of a wood-burning heater.

One thing you should know, though, is that it's not as easy as

Max makes it look. "I been practicing a lot, so it looks easy, but it's not. This has got six *sentidos a la vez*.

"You got this leg in time on the cymbal, that's one. This leg with the drum, that's two. This hand on the guitar that's doin' the chords is three, and this other hand that's playin', that's four. You got your mind thinkin' what to do, that's five. And then when you sing, that's six—six senses all at once!"

And all this at an age when many of his contemporaries are losing rather than gaining senses. But age has never been much of a factor for Max—he worked well past retirement age, and not in some *oficina*, but as an ironworker. In fact, he was reinforcing iron at a California construction site back in 1975 when he injured his back.

"I belong to the union, but soon as I get hurt, the union threw me out. They say I couldn't work no more," Max says. Of course, by the time the union "threw him out," Max was nearly seventy. But he wasn't about to sit down on his pension, so this father of twelve children decided to move back to his native mountains with his wife, Juanita, and, as he puts it, "get busy."

And if you want to know just how busy he's been, you've got to do more than catch one of his one-man concerts. You've also got to tour the Trujillo Gallery and Polycultural Center on the main drag through Taos and see the more than one hundred artistic creations Max has on display. He does everything—painting, carving, cabinetwork, metal sculpture, ironwork—you name it. And, as you might expect, he creates it all "since scratch."

Take his paintings, for instance. Not only does Max construct his own frames out of weathered and worm-eaten lumber from discarded ladders and doors, but he also creates his own paints. No one taught him how—he just "picked 'em up."

"I make 'em all with dirt, glue, and sawdust. This red here is from some red dirt from Utah. The white is *tierra blanca*—I get that up by Ojo, by the hot springs. Here's cedar wood ground up—I mix that with dirt, too."

The black comes from *hollín*—the soot Max scrapes from his stovepipes—and the green is extracted from fresh alfalfa. But those screaming yellows and electric blues? Well, Max cooked up a way to create those colors, too, and what the process might lack in tradition, it makes up for in flair. The pragmatic artist simply grinds up his grandchildren's crayolas, screens them, and mixes them with his clay base.

Who would ever conceive of doing such a thing, you ask? Take a stroll through the gallery, and you'll find yourself repeating the question. Max's artistic technique is unschooled, but it's also refreshingly unfettered. This is art as great fun, and the artist invites you to join in the play.

Max's painting of his childhood home is a good example. In it the Luz O. Trujillo house sits above an old *molino,* a water mill whose logs are built up with layers of Max's earthen paint. It's impossible to resist touching this canvas so full of textures and surprises, like the actual minuscule leaves glued into the trees above the mill.

Max's rendition of the Ranchos de Taos Church reflects an even more novel approach. The church is painted with a genuine mud plaster, complete with tiny, golden flecks of wheat straw. The *vigas* and *canales* of the church actually protrude from the surface of the painting, jolting your normal sense of perspective and making you see the famed church in a wholly different way.

That same freshness of vision characterizes Max's carvings and sculptures as well. Consider that aspen chest with the handmade iron hinges and clasps, for instance. It's a casket, actually, and when Max is asked what led him to create a *cajón de muerte,* he replies by lifting the lid to expose a life-size carving of a buried Christ, *un santo entierro.*

"This one here, he's already usin' it," Max smiles, gesturing at the heavily bearded, skeletal *Cristo* laid to rest in a cushion of lacy ex-curtains.

There's another Christ next to the coffin, this one a handcarved *bulto* of a crucifixion. One of the most striking features of the unorthodox *santo* is its scraggly locks of real human hair. And where did Max find *ese cabello tan largo?*

"From the barber shop. They cut lots of hippie hair around here, you know," he replies brightly.

But there aren't only figures of Christ in the Trujillo Gallery and Polycultural Center. Max's art is as eclectic as his music, and just a short distance from the occupied *cajón de muerte* is a chained pit bull carved from the fork of an apple tree. The black-and-white dog with his Styrofoam-pellet hide stares balefully through agate eyes that seem to follow you as you walk past. Farther on, the viewer encounters an oversize *carreta de muerte.* But the figure of Death that rides in this Penitente death cart is not the usual anthropomorphic *Comadre Sebastiana* with her empty stare and rigor mortis grin. Max's *Muerte,* a cow skeleton he found while gathering piñon in Carson National Forest, is duly horrific, yet the addition of a real cow's tail at the tip of the bony spine gives this Death figure a decidedly daffy demeanor.

There are comparable surprises around every corner; the gallery is a full-steam celebration of creativity. Here are tin candelabras, an apple crusher, *retablos* of San Rafael, coffee tables, jewelry chests with handmade locks, paintings of jungle parrots on deerskin framed in elaborately scrolled wrought iron, and a collection of Max's specially designed guitars, including a big-bellied *guitarrón* and an electric bass fashioned out of a brass bell.

One of my personal favorites, though, is Max's latest painting, which hangs in a place of honor back home at his workshop. A handcarved burro and an elephant are fastened to a painted back-drop of mountains. Two strings hang from the bottom of the piece that, as Max demonstrates, can be manipulated to make the political animals rear.

And as the artist "pulls the strings" just like all those notori-ous *patrones* of the north, I reflect on how this mobile painting is a typical Max Trujillo creation. It's playful and inventive and made "since scratch"—and, yes, it really works, all six *sentidos a la vez.*

FLORENCE NARANJO

his one was handed down to me by my grandmother," Florence Naranjo of San Ildefonso Pueblo says, fingering a sepia-colored polishing stone. The teardrop agate, which has been used to burnish three generations of black pottery, is one of Florence's favorites. She prefers the timeworn stone just as she prefers her traditional way of life. "I'm still the same," she says—"still doing everything the old way."

Born at Picurís Pueblo in 1921, Florence was one of nine children of Rosalie and José Angel Aguilar, themselves well-known potters. Florence learned the art of pottery making from her paternal grandmother, Susana, at the age of ten. But she couldn't make much pottery during her youth, as she attended boarding school in Santa Fe until her graduation in 1940. "I wanted to continue my schooling—to go into nursing," Florence recalls, "but my parents didn't have enough money to send me." And so the young woman returned to San Ildefonso and began working in Los Alamos. But then she met Louis Naranjo of Santa Clara Pueblo; the couple was married, and Florence began raising the family that would ultimately include three sons and two daughters.

"But tell them your first husband's name!" Louis calls from his seat in front of the television in the living room, adding, "You better be ready to write another article, 'cause we're gettin' a divorce next week."

Florence, of course, is still married to her "first husband," and there's no more chance that she'll divorce him than there is that he'll ever stop teasing her. Louis, who has worked in Los Alamos for some twenty years, also participates in the creation of the fine black pots. "I make the pottery and polish it," Florence explains, "and Louis paints it." It's a tradition that comes down from Florence's own parents—her mother and father also split the labor in a similar fashion.

The entire process of pottery making at San Ildefonso Pueblo is similarly guided by tradition and has remained virtually unchanged since the time of Florence's grandparents. The potter must first, of course, collect her clay; Florence finds her red clay both in her own pueblo and in surrounding villages. She then soaks the clay for two days, after which she combines it with a finely sieved white sand she collects in the Pojoaque area. Once she has mixed her clay satisfactorily, Florence begins constructing her pot. Working on a saucer as a base, she builds coils up, allowing them to set for some fifteen or twenty minutes before shaping them out. Florence, as per custom, uses a gourd to fashion the walls of her pots. "If you want higher pots," she explains, "you have to put on more coils." But she cautions that you cannot immediately work the coils up—you must be patient and allow the lower base to set.

It's a time-consuming process, especially if you want the delicate, thin walls Florence is able to achieve in her finely crafted creations. Yet, once Florence has shaped her pot, the work has only begun. Next, she must smooth the piece, initially with a fine grade of sandpaper, followed by a wet cloth. Then comes the most painstaking procedure of all—the polishing. The potter chooses one or more stones from her highly prized collection to polish the pot. She must rub and rub, and then rub some more until all the surfaces of the pot are evenly burnished.

After the pot has been polished, it's time for the designing and painting. Husband Louis prepares his paint from a natural white clay slip gathered from the La Bajada area. He paints the outlines of the design with a yucca brush and fills in the large areas with a standard paintbrush. "Mostly he paints the feather design," Florence explains. "Some potters also do the water serpent, but the feather's the most traditional design in San Ildefonso, so we stick to it."

Florence no longer carves out a design in her pots, commenting that the painted pattern is more traditional. She credits her mother, however, with first developing the process of carving a design in black pottery. "The first piece she did that way is at the Denver Museum now," she says. After her mother's innovation, Florence remarks, everybody started carving designs. "Santa Clara just used to do the hand print—the bear claw, but now they do etching, too."

But, whether etched or painted, the pot must finally be fired. This is perhaps the most delicate procedure of all, yet it is the secret to the rich color of the black pots. First, Florence props up a sheet of iron with tin cans. She places firewood under the plate and stacks the pottery on top. The pots are then covered with roofing tin and a layer of dried cow patties, and the wood is ignited. "When the fire dies down a little, we put horse manure on top," Florence says, indicating that the carbonizing effect of the smoke is what imbues the pots with their rich color, though the potter must be careful not to leave the clay pieces in the fire too long. Florence can't give the precise amount of time the pots must remain in the fire; like a master chef, she needs no recipe—"I just know when they're ready."

And that she does.

If you have any doubts, just ask the judges at the Santa Fe Indian Market, the Gallup Indian Ceremonial, or the Eight Northern Pueblos Show. Florence has taken home ribbons for her pottery from all three. Or you might ask the customers who come from all corners of the county, tracking the potter down and knocking at her door, which has red and blue corn hanging on it, only to find, more often than not, that she's busy filling back orders.

All this activity might sound like quite enough to keep a grandmother of twelve busy, but it's only a part of Florence's artistic life. She's also a weaver and has received awards for her woven creations, too, including "Best of Pueblo Weaving" at the Santa Fe Indian Market. "When I'm not doing pottery, I'm weaving," Florence says, and it's a balance that seems to work out well. During the warm season, she makes pottery, but when the weather turns cold, she can be found behind her loom in the wood-heated adobe studio Louis built out behind the house during a strike in Los Alamos.

"I have a *Two Grey Hills* on the loom now," Florence says, gesturing at the intricate design. And the cross-cultural implications of the weaving are nearly as complex and intertwined as the grey and brown geometric pattern itself. Here is a Pueblo weaver using a Spanish-style floor loom to create a Navajo rug for an Anglo buyer. And all this several centuries after the Navajos, who first learned how to weave from the Pueblos, began using the wool first introduced by the Spaniards to ultimately build such a strong market for their work that many people nowadays believe the Pueblos never had a weaving tradition at all.

But, whether her buyers understand the history of her weaving tradition or not, Florence does know the world of those buyers quite well. She lectures and gives demonstrations at Bandelier National Monument and in the Los Alamos schools. She's also a longtime member of the San Ildefonso School Board and a regular participant in leadership workshops.

Yet, Florence is, even more essentially, a traditional Pueblo woman. And it is her Pueblo obligations that remain at the center of her life. Feast days are the most important times in the Pueblo calendar, and the San Ildefonso feast day on January 23 is a major event in Florence's year.

Early on the morning of that day, the outlines of furtive deer appear on the hills surrounding the pueblo. Only when they descend in the crisp dawn light is the observer able to shake the illusion of having seen actual fleet-footed animals instead of deer *dancers*.

Though Florence herself has danced on feast day, she now leaves the dancing to her children and grandchildren. But the preparation of the food—that cannot be delegated. Florence uses seventy-five pounds of flour to make the bread alone, and much more is needed to bake the mountains of *bizcochitos* and the numerous prune pies. Then beans, *chicos,* and rich, red chile must be prepared in massive quantities, as well as the indispensable garbanzo stew. "We invite everyone in to eat," Florence says, describing the familiar Pueblo custom. "Sometimes we don't even know the people, but still we invite them in."

Other important events in San Ildefonso's cultural calendar include a spring Easter dance. In this unique dance, which is not done every year, there are only two women who dance with a gourd while a much larger group of men dance around them. "These two ladies inherit their part in the dance from their families," Florence says, indicating she has been one of the participants in this special dance.

And then there is the Corn Dance, which is performed on September 6. Florence has photos of the last Corn Dance, and she proudly points out two of her young grandchildren in the rows of dancers. One day Florence will hand down her grandmother's polishing stone to one of those grandchildren. And she knows they will, in turn, keep the "old way" alive and those black pots shining for generations to come.

FATHER JOSÉ TERES

e looks like a latter-day Methuselah, with his mottled, leathery skin and his turtle eyes blinking venerably through prismatic eyeglasses. There's not much vision left to correct in those nearly sightless eyes, and his hearing is almost totally gone. Yet, Father José Teres eats well, moves with remarkable ease, and still says mass every day as he has for eighty years. His mind is honed, his memory sharp, and his gravelly voice retains authority as well as a constant readiness to overflow into laughter.

Not bad for a man planning to celebrate his one hundred and fifth birthday—a man who was born on the seventeenth day of the seventh month of the seventy-seventh year—of the previous century.

"I told him I'd take him to the Downs at Santa Fe on his birthday so he could bet on number seven," chuckles Father José Cubells, Teres's former student and lifelong companion. Fr. Cubells likes to laugh even more than his mentor, but, then, he's still a youngster at a mere seventy-eight years of age.

As we sit in the living room of the rectory at the Santa Cruz Church, next door to the massive *iglesia* that itself has been standing for two and one-half centuries, we become witnesses to the rare relationship between the two elderly priests. Fr. Cubells speaks with warmth and respect about the *anciano* he cares for "like our *niño*." Then, in the next breath, he teases the centenarian, joking that Fr. Teres has shown up this morning with all his medals on, even his Purple Heart.

Sometimes, though, life with Fr. Teres can be difficult, as the old man is independent and extremely headstrong, but that's part of the relationship, too. *"A veces nos hace enfadar,* but that's life," Fr. Cubells observes bilingually, dissolving into his characteristic *risa* once again.

That robust sense of self-reliance has been a way of life for the *padre* who was born in Vellvis, in the province of Lleida, Spain. Fr. Teres entered the Seminary of the Sons of the Holy Family and was ordained as a priest in Barcelona in 1904. This priestly order had been founded only three years before by Joseph Manyante i Vives. And some eighty years later, Fr. Teres made an incredible journey back to Spain, completely on his own at one hundred and one years of age, to testify to the heroic virtues of the founder of his order.

The church is in the process of beatifying the founding priest, whom Fr. Teres not only knew but also lived with for some time. Beatification is the second phase in a three-step elevation to sainthood, Cubells explains, adding that Teres has told him that their founder may have been a saint, but "he put me in the corner several times, too."

After Fr. Teres's ordination, he became a mathematics instructor, teaching algebra for thirty years in several schools in Catalonia, including an orphanage school where he was an administrator. It was in such a boarding school where Fr. Cubells, then a fourteen year old from the Catalonian town of Tarragona, first met Fr. Teres, who was his teacher. "I remember it was in 1913, during the war, and Fr. Teres made a windmill for us. We had planted potatoes and had to raise water for them, so he made the windmill. All by himself."

But, as Fr. Cubells explains, Fr. Teres has always done things for himself. In 1927, he ventured across the Atlantic to Santa Cruz, New Mexico, after one of the first priests of the Sons of the Holy Family order, Agustín Vilalta, died in a horse accident. Since the Santa Cruz parish covered such a huge geographic area, priests had to travel in a horse and *bogue* to the outlying missions from Truchas all the way to Nambé. "Fr. Vilalta used to ride with the reins behind his neck," Fr. Cubells recounts the story. "Once, on a turn, he was thrown out, and the buggy and the horses rolled over him."

After serving a brief period of time in Santa Cruz, Fr. Teres journeyed to Del Norte and Greeley, Colorado, where he spent many years. From there, he traveled to Gardner, Colorado, where he was pastor for seven years. *"Había muy poca gente allí, muy pobre,"* Fr. Teres remembers—"There were very few people there, and they were extremely poor. So I left because I told myself, here you are going to die of hunger!"

Following his "escape from Gardner," as Fr. Teres puts it, he went to the San Joaquin valley in California for two years, after which he finally returned to his home parish in Santa Cruz. During all those years, the industrious priest built several *capillas,* including the chapel he constructed himself in Colorado. "He was a great carpenter," Fr. Cubells notes. "He even made a metal bell tower for that *capilla* and, when everyone was afraid to put it up, he put it up there himself."

Fr. Teres was also responsible for renovating the two side rooms at the famous Santuario de Chimayó. *"Parecía un corral,"* Fr. Cubells says—"It looked like a corral. Cattle and horses would walk in and out, but Fr. Teres fixed the rooms up with his own hands. He was also a good mechanic. He could take an engine apart and put it back together, piece by piece."

The elderly priest also drove his own car until his mid-eighties. Fr. Cubells recalls how the State Motor Vehicle Division finally refused Fr. Teres a license because of his failing eyesight. But Fr. Cubells, in an effort to spare the feelings of the proud old *padre,* made an arrangement with the government agency to write Fr. Teres an annual letter informing him that his application for a license was still "under consideration."

"Year after year, they'd send that same letter, and Fr. Teres would say, 'Anytime now.' "

But Fr. Teres doesn't need a license to walk, and he does so "all night long," according to Fr. Cubells, who notes that the *anciano* sleeps most of the day. But today is an exception to that rule, and Fr. Teres does step very lively as he travels down the hall, nearly leaving Fr. Cubells behind. "Yes, he goes jogging up and down here all the time!" the younger priest jokes.

It is inevitable, however, that sometimes Fr. Teres gets into trouble due to his near-blindness. Fr. Cubells locks all the exterior doors to keep the *anciano* from wandering off into the night. But there are plenty of hazards within the rectory itself, and Fr. Teres details the story of how he decided to go to the basement for a soft drink one evening four or five months ago. The ancient priest lost his footing in the darkness and fell ten steps down to the concrete floor. Incredibly, he wasn't badly hurt. In fact, Fr. Cubells observes, the indestructible *viejito* walked back up the steps by himself—and with the drink in his hand!

"*Este hombre tiene una constitución de hierro*," Fr. Cubells shakes his head—"This man has an iron constitution. Even the devil is afraid of him!"

Once, Fr. Cubells remembers, Fr. Teres burned himself with the blessed sacrament candle on the small private altar in the living room where he usually says mass. "Yet, within ten days, his burned hand had healed," Fr. Cubells says, noting that his one-hundred-four-year-old *compañero* eats well—"better than I do, in fact." The *anciano* eats three full meals a day, including the supper he prepares himself, a soup made out of boiled eggs, toast, garlic, and milk.

"*Sopa hervida alarga la vida*," Fr. Cubells mirthfully cites the old Spanish *dicho*. "Boiled soup prolongs life," the proverb translates, and the living proof sits before us.

Not that Fr. Cubells himself isn't amazingly energetic and healthy in his late seventies. He's also led a very active priestly life, which began when he followed Fr. Teres to the United States. After a brief stay in Del Norte, Colorado, he settled into the parish of Santa Cruz. From 1930 to 1941, Fr. Cubells commuted on weekends to the CCC camps in the Frijoles Canyon and to the Los Alamos Ranch School. He was the first priest to say mass in what was to become the "atomic city," and he knew Robert Oppenheimer well.

During World War II, Fr. Cubells served in an army chapel in Argentina, and afterwards at Walter Reed Army Center. "Eisenhower was there, and I visited several times with him and Mrs. Eisenhower, too," the priest remembers. Finally, he returned, like his old teacher, to his home parish of Santa Cruz, where he's been for thirty years.

While Fr. Cubells has been elaborating on his own life, the nearly deaf Fr. Teres has delivered a monologue about his childhood in Spain, principally talking about his father, who was a pharmacist. As a hobby, the elder Teres distilled the sour wine farmers would bring to him. "They'd go back home with big bottles of anisette," I hear Fr. Teres say at one point, but much is lost in the confusing counterpoint of two simultaneous stories about different centuries on separate sides of the Atlantic.

"*Donde hay dos españoles, hay tres opiniones*," Fr. Cubells laughs— "Where there are two Spaniards, there are three opinions."

But, speaking of anisette, wouldn't we like to sample a little Spanish brandy? Though Fr. Teres has claimed he never drinks, Fr. Cubells gently corrects the record, noting that the *anciano* does like a touch of liqueur in his coffee.

Fr. Cubells pours us a taste of Fundador brandy while I ask Fr. Teres if he has any desire to return to his native Spain. "No," he replies. "After fifty-five years in this country, *soy más gringo que español*."

And he is acculturated—worldly-wise, you might say. Recently, a television crew from Albuquerque filmed him, but Fr. Teres was hardly star-struck by all the attention. "Oh, he doesn't care. *Está curado de sustos*," Fr. Cubells exclaims in a colorful expression— "He's been cured of every fright."

But what shall we drink to? Long life would surely seem appropriate, but Fr. Cubells has a better idea, recalling a story he's told earlier in the conversation. There had, at one time, been talk about the possibility of Fr. Teres having to go into a nursing home. Fr. Cubells addressed that issue in his homily at the Mass celebrating Fr. Teres's one-hundredth birthday several years ago. He described the nursing homes he had seen—"the old ladies and men in the waiting room, sleeping, crying, floundering their eyes. And I said, if Fr. Teres would come to this place, instead of a 'waiting room,' this would become a 'living room'—a thing of life."

So that is the toast to which we raise our glasses—"a 'living room,' not a 'waiting room.' " And I can't imagine a room anywhere more full of life.

MARCOS GÓMEZ

hey appeared one morning—the men with the tripods and the squinty eyes— and they didn't ask permission to drive stakes into the land that had been Marcos Gómez's home since his birth.

"I told my daddy, 'I think the government's coming.' He said, 'No, they can't come in here.' And I said, 'Yes, they can. *El gobierno puede tirar nuestro monte si quiere*—The government can throw down our mountains if it wants to.' "

Don Marcos didn't realize just how accurate his words were, for those surveyors tramping across his family's *rancho* on the high mesas of Los Alamos were staking out the boundaries of the Manhattan Project—the project to develop the first atomic weapon. Of course, don Marcos and his *vecinos* had no idea at the time that their mountains would be used by men who would unlock a force powerful enough to, indeed, *tirar el monte*. All they knew was that they were being evicted by a government that gave them a check for their condemned land, but which took away something no amount of money could recompense—their traditional way of life.

After losing their land, don Marcos and his wife, María, migrated to the Española valley, settling into doña María's native *pueblito* of Alcalde. Don Marcos purchased as much *terreno* as he could with his government payoff, but the plot of land was too small to support his growing family, so the lifelong *ranchero* ended up working, ironically enough, for the very *gobierno* that had evicted him. Bussed up the same hill where his home had been, don Marcos joined the ranks of the army of laborers hired to construct the "atomic city."

Don Marcos considers himself lucky in a sense: he was able to make the transition from a land-based subsistence lifestyle to the new "money economy"—he worked hard, became bilingual, and survived. Some members of the older generation, however, were unable to make such a drastic adjustment; don Marcos's own mother was among them.

"Mama died shortly after we lost the ranch," he recalls. "*Se puso triste, muy triste*—She got sad, very sad, and she became sick all the time. *Se le hizo muy duro salir del rancho*—It was very hard on her to leave the ranch."

It was hard on don Marcos as well, but he relied on his sense of humor to get by, a ready wit that made him the equal to any tricks life might play on him, and more than eighty years of living haven't dulled his sharpness. "I'm four years old," the *anciano* says—"I just don't count all the years that come after that." Actually, he was born on April 25 in 1903, this man who savors laughter and labels himself an "April fool."

"*Mi vida ha sido el rancho*," he says with pride—"My life has been the land. I've been a *ranchero*, a sheepherder, and a cowboy."

And it's those early years on the family ranch on Pajarito Mesa that the *viejito* still remembers most fondly. The work was back-breaking, he says, but the land was fertile and there was never a shortage of water. "*Más antes sí caiba agua*," don Marcos says, echoing the sentiment of many northern *ancianos*—"In the old days, it really used to rain. It would rain for weeks at a time, until the water would start leaking through the roof. '*El tiempo de las goteras*' we used to call it—'The time of the drops.' "

But even when it didn't rain, there were always the *ojitos*, the natural springs in the mountain canyons that ranchers could use for watering their livestock. The Gómez family, in fact, used to draw water for their own consumption from such an *ojito* located below their home. The elder recalls how hard it was to carry buckets of water up the steep incline to his house—that is, until he and one of his brothers came up with the idea of constructing a wooden sled that allowed them to slide an entire barrel of water up the hill at once.

There was no way, however, to rig an easier ride up that much larger hill from the Española valley to the mesa-top ranch. As don Marcos recalls it, the family didn't make that *viaje* too often— didn't have to, since they raised nearly everything they needed on their self-sufficient *rancho*. But there were some necessities the land could not provide, and the *viejito* still remembers loading up three pack mules with sacks of beans and peas in order to make the difficult thirteen-mile trek down into the valley. Don Marcos would sell those peas for a quarter a bushel and the *frijoles* for a dollar and a half a hundred-pound sack. Then he'd buy what he needed at the old Bond General Store at the Chili Line depot. "We'd only buy the things we couldn't harvest ourselves—*aceite de lámpara, fósforos, azúcar, café*—kerosene, matches, sugar, and coffee."

When don Marcos wasn't behind a team of horses in the fields, he was usually up in the Valle Grande *cuidando borregas*. But sheepherding was no pastoral pastime—it was a difficult job and dangerous, too, with all those predators hidden in the pines. There were mountain lions and the inevitable coyotes, not to mention an occasional bear. Yet, don Marcos claims he was never afraid of *osos*. "*Si uno no los molesta, no molestan a uno tampoco*," he says—"If you don't bother them, they won't bother you either." Of course, there were times when man and beast stumbled upon each other, which was why don Marcos always kept his rifle close at hand. And he was called upon to use it once, too, he recalls, when he decided to bed down in a cave already occupied by a bear.

But the worst predator was the wolf, don Marcos says, explaining that what makes *lobos* particularly dangerous is the fact that they always run in packs. "But *you* better not run when wolves are around," he cautions, "or they'll get you for sure." It's also certain they'll get plenty of *borregas* as well, and don Marcos still remembers the time he lost three hundred head of sheep to a pack of wolves. "It was more than they could eat—they killed them just to kill them."

Another wild creature feared and abhorred by most served as a childhood pet for don Marcos. The *viejito* used to catch rattlesnakes and keep them in homemade cages. "*Soy como los del jungle*," he exclaims. "I used to pick *víboras* up with my hands." Feeding the captive snakes was no problem, don Marcos says, explaining how he used to fill empty *saquitos* of Duke tobacco with wheat. He'd place the sacks in the cage as bait for mice, which, in turn, would provide a steady supply of food for his snakes.

Don Marcos also found ingenious ways to entertain himself with his pet *víboras*. "I used to tie sardine cans together with string and make the snakes carry them around," he laughs. But it was no laughing matter when a hired hand who worked for the boy's father killed the snakes one day. "I cried all day long," the *anciano* remembers.

Still, the vast majority of the memories from those days when there was no electricity on the hill—much less particle accelerators and X-ray lasers—bring a smile to don Marcos's wizened face. And the most beautiful thing about the past, he says without reservation, was the sense of community among the people.

"*En aquellos tiempos, toda la vecindad se juntaba*," he observes— "Back in those times, all the neighbors would get together. People would say, 'Come over and have dinner with us.' And there would be the *viejitos* with their *atole*, with their *frijoles y chilito*."

Along with that sense of community came a strong tradition of respect, especially for one's elders. "In those days, if an elder told you to get something for them, you'd go running. Not anymore. *Ahora si se van, no vuelven*—Now, if they go, they don't come back."

Don Marcos himself always dreamed of someday coming back to the family ranch he lost to the government, if only for a brief visit. It took more than thirty years and a petition to the White House before he finally got that chance to set foot on the land that had once been his. And though the 1975 visit was a moving personal experience for don Marcos and his wife, it was anything but private. Not only was the couple accompanied by the obligatory entourage of lab security guards, but they were also followed by a film crew and CBS News correspondent Charles Kuralt, who interviewed don Marcos for a report on homesteading. Family photographs of the occasion show a rather forlorn looking don Marcos wearing a battered hat and an oversize badge reading, "Pass 101— Uncleared Visitor, Escort Required." He and his wife stand stiffly under the frozen ponderosas in the snow-dusted ruins of the log cabin that had once been their home. Don Marcos holds the cast-iron headboard of his parents' bed, the only souvenir of the past he could find to take home.

It was only after the security passes were surrendered and

Charles Kuralt was well down the road to his next assignment that this "uncleared visitor" and his wife finally expressed their emotions over their long-awaited homecoming. "When we got back, we both just sat down and cried—*lloramos los dos*," don Marcos says, slowly shutting the photo album.

ANNA SOPYN

h no!'' Anna Sopyn throws up her earth-stained hands in protest when we request she put her arm around her husband, John, for a picture.

"Now look like you like me," John says with a toothless grin as the couple stands together on the shaded steps of Sopyn's Fruit Stand in Rinconada. "Like American wife now. Today kiss me, tomorrow make fight."

Anna, whose eyes widen as she holds the pose for a full two seconds, suddenly bolts away, bellowing, "Too much, too *much*!"

But not before we have captured the aging couple in a classic New Mexican Gothic pose between the tomatoes and the peaches.

It was a rare moment, for the enormously energetic Anna has again become a blur of activity, rearranging the already perfect pyramids of peaches. A woman of constant motion, Anna even sways as she speaks, hacking away at the sky with an inexhaustible array of gestures.

She hasn't sat still in the thirty years since she and her husband arrived in these fruitful highlands of northern New Mexico with literally nothing but the clothes on their backs. "Don't got even ten cents," as John remembers it. The year was 1951, and the couple was a world away from their native Russia.

"Come America," Anna waves her arms in two directions at once, "with just eight-months baby. No penny, no nothing. I don't know what to do. I'm comin', I'm scared. I don't understand talk. I'm thinkin' I still might go back."

Anna, of course, didn't go back. The Sopyns overcame their linguistic and financial handicaps through hard work and, as Anna fondly recalls, the generosity of their newfound neighbors in this small community tucked between Taos and Embudo.

"A lot of the neighbors help, takin' me to town, takin' me everywhere. And they're puttin' jerky in a basket, baby food, twenty-five cents, fifty, and I buy groceries, and I'm so happy, uh-hum. I'm appreciative what they doin' for me."

The Sopyns, however, did not survive by the charity of their neighbors but, rather, by working for them. "My husband work day and night for everyone," Anna says, still fussing with the peaches, removing a bruised one and depositing it beneath a rough table glittering with quarters. "Two and a half years workin' in store. I'm dishes washin' and he in store. Sixty dollars for both a month, and give lunch. But I happy, I'm workin' hard."

John gazes at the table full of coins—this man who is said to have purchased his first pickup truck with the wadded fives and ones from the family fruit stand—and remembers his first days as a *nuevomexicano*. "No *sabe* speak English, no *sabe* nothin'," the trilingual Russian says in a bilingual expression that is pure northern New Mexico.

"At first I work for all the people. I no workin' eight hours, ten hours. *Sixteen* hours I work! And someone tell me—ha, ha, *you* crazy, you workin' so much. Now they tellin' me, you rich man. I tell them, how come *you* not rich? You speak language, you have school. But I work hard. I *born* workin'. You not workin', you not makin' this kind of peach."

John holds up a large crimson specimen as proof of what he's saying, but there's evidence enough in the simple fact that, within six years, the penniless couple was able to purchase the farm they still cultivate today. It was hard work, but then the life the Sopyns had left behind in the old country had been even harder. Both were born in the Ukranian city of Kiev, where, as Anna recalls, "everybody work for government. And you no complain—huh-uh. You complain—*more* bad."

Anna and John, however, didn't have to complain in order for things to get "more bad." Hitler took care of that in 1942 when the Nazis invaded and occupied the Sopyns' homeland, forcing the Ukranians into exile and compulsory labor in Germany.

"In Germany, they move you, move like dogs. Another place, another place—Stuttgart, Munich—you can't stay. I ask, why you takin' me? Had to go work. Two years workin'. No pay, nothin'. I no like," Anna says with considerable understatement.

The forced labor and exile finally came to an end with the signing of the armistice, but the uprooted couple would never return home again. When they were offered a contract from an American to come and work in the United States, the Sopyns eagerly accepted, crossing the ocean and eventually arriving in northern New Mexico with nothing in their pockets and with an eight-month-old baby named Valentina.

Valentina is grown now, as are the Sopyns' three other children, and those bitter memories of servitude under the Nazis seem more than an ocean and a half century away as Anna drives a bright blue Ford 3000 tractor past the cherry and apricot trees over freshly cut orchard grass. Yet, life wasn't so easy here either in the early days as the couple worked round the clock for six years to save the money to purchase their farm. And once they did buy the property in 1957, they had to work even harder to make it productive.

"Thirty years day and night we work, and nothin' with tractor. All the time, push, push," Anna says, simulating the operation of a hand-driven plow. The orchard also had to be built up. "It was an old orchard, only old trees. Every penny I'm plantin' trees, plantin' trees. I'm pretty worried. They die, I plant new ones. I can't tell you how many trees."

Anna does know, however, that this year she planted 170 new peach trees, though she adds, "This is last time. If they die, I don't plant no more. So hard life. Kids start growin' and help, but now all run away and leave old people."

Here Anna has slipped into hyperbole, for son Greg is working with his parents and, in fact, appeared earlier this afternoon when his mother was picking tomatoes, hunched sturdily over the rows of plants with a bucket tied to a rag around her waist. As Anna wiped the sweat from the edge of a red bandana tied around her greying swatch of hair, mother and son engaged in a Russian and English conversation that seemed perfectly appropriate in this code-switching land.

And Anna hardly looks too old to be planting trees. Born in 1920, her face is furrowed by long years in the sun, but her movements all telegraph strength. She is missing a majority of her teeth, but not a bit of her spirit, which continues to burn in her eyes, always on the verge of erupting in a burst of verbal and bodily language—just as it does when we ask how long she and John have been married. "Oh, I want to *forget*!" she roars, flinging her arms skyward.

But, all histrionics aside, Anna probably would just as soon forget the last year she spent nursing her critically ill husband back to health. "One year ago, he so sick," Anna begins the story, explaining that the doctor believed John's illness might have been caused by exposure to insecticides. "Two months hospital in Santa Fe. Doctor said wasn't' gonna live. I said, I'm takin' home. Every machine takin' off. Start feed him with spoon. At first, spoon. Spritz I'm feedin' him. Got pneumonia. Kids say, takin' hospital, can't get better."

But John did get better with Anna's attention, and the elderly man, whose weight had nosedived to a mere eighty pounds, began to recover. In the meantime, though, John's legs had atrophied, forcing him to undergo physical therapy at St. Joseph Hospital. Again, the prognosis was dim. The doctors said he might never walk again, but Anna had other ideas.

"Start exercisin' him," she says. "Now in wheelchair. Start with walker. And after, startin' with cane—uh-hum. Then, throw cane away. And he all right, startin' eat. And now—*startin' smokin'*!"

The last observation is delivered with Anna's typical explosion of harried arm gestures, as if not only her mind but her entire body were rebelling against the absurdity of it all: the feeble husband who nearly widowed her puffing on a Lucky Strike while she's still planting peach trees, which she ought to be irrigating right now instead of posing for pictures and talking all day about Russia.

"Too much—*too much*!" Anna complains. Anyway, that's all in the past—the old family forgotten, the old country no more than a fading memory. John only has two living brothers left in Russia, but he never writes them because he fears it might endanger their jobs. Anna also has largely lost touch with her surviving siblings, though she does get an occasional letter from her sister, urging her to return to her homeland.

"My sister says lots better there now. Says, why not comin' home? But I'm not goin' back. There I'm nothin'. Here, I have something."

And what the Sopyns have they have been working hard for all their lives. You not workin', you not makin' this kind of peach.

PAUL PACHECO

here's a fine line between life and death, a tenuous thread separating spirituality and the theater of the absurd. Meet Paul Pacheco of Española and walk that line.

There are miracles and mountains of overturned bicycles and mistaken burials and Matachines Dances in this story, but no deus ex machina. The "god" in this case is *in* the machine. The wooden figure of Christ that Paul claims miraculously appeared at his house is in an antique wagon with oversize iron wheels. The white-faced *santo* with the black beard, thorny crown, and cross slung over his shoulder came complete with a self-contained lighting system to illuminate him at night, though the wiring has long since decayed.

At the head of the wagon is a handcarved wooden post with a rusty light socket. A frayed electric wire hangs uselessly from the black box that once held a six-volt battery to supply the juice needed to light up the face of Christ. Paul supplied the white clothing for the saint, who, he says, came dressed up originally in red. The elder also built the frame around the *santo's* head, which looks like a gutted television set and hangs at a precarious angle ever since those mischievous neighborhood kids came with their BB guns to blow out the glass.

There was an earlier time, Paul says, when priests and pilgrims came instead of *muchachos malcriados*. They came from all parts of New Mexico and Colorado to visit the *capilla* Paul built during the early 1940s for his saint. The rock arch of the shrine that protects the rosary-clad *Cristo* also houses a small army of other saints, which Paul says were donated by visiting *peregrinos*. It's a rather bedraggled army now, as most of the gessoed statues are missing a limb or two—or even a head.

One of the plaster of paris heads sits forlornly and strangely watchful on a ledge beneath a bouquet of pink and yellow plastic roses, its eyes skewed to one side as if it were scrutinizing you out of the corner of its eyes. Nearby is a curious black crucifix with a metallic Christ, red light bulbs, and reflectors from a child's bicycle. The crucifix is housed in a wooden box with blistered white paint, above which someone has stuck a plastic Little Miss Muppet watering her daisies with a huge watering can.

Also in the shrine are several of the wooden crosses Paul is best known for. Though the eighty-five-year-old man says his arthritic hands don't allow him to work any longer, he once supplied many a grave site with the colorful *cruces*. Each cross is unique: some sport carved hearts and others are crowned with stars, but they all feature tiers of red and blue routed circles the size of a mason jar lid.

It was probably inevitable that this Española native should end up fashioning crosses for *sepulturas*—he's always enjoyed tinkering in his shop, and he's had a rather special relationship with death.

"It was in 1918," the *anciano* begins as he settles back into his weathered recliner in the shade of a huge cottonwood, "the year of the big influenza. They were burying the dead right away *para que no prendiera la enfermedad*—so that the disease wouldn't spread. I got sick like everybody did, and one day I fainted. I guess they thought I was dead, so they buried me. But the good thing was they didn't bury me in a coffin. *Me enterraron en un sarape*—They buried me in a blanket.

"When I woke up, I found myself in the ground, so I started digging as fast as I could until I got out of there."

You can still see the place where Paul claims he was buried alive; the hole, in fact, is located directly in front of the shrine. That *pozo* is covered now with rotting planks and the carcasses of several lawn chairs, but it's the spot where Paul wants to be buried when he actually dies. "I was born and raised here, and this is where I want to stay," he declares as his four miniature white dogs frolic over his aging lap.

As one might expect, Paul has no fear of dying, and that's not only because he's already been through a burial. From his earliest years he was forced to come face-to-face with fear. When he was only nine years old, he says, he left school and took a ten-dollar-a-month job herding sheep in Tierra Amarilla.

"I'd sleep up there in the mountains with the sheep," he recalls. "Everybody would say, *'Qué padre tan malo que te tiene aquí donde te pueden comer los coyotes*—What a mean father you have, sending you up here where you might get eaten by coyotes.' But I'd tell them, no, it's my own idea—not his. I was never scared once—*A mí nunca me daba miedo.*"

In the more than seventy years since then, Paul has never been afraid to do just what he pleased. A former repairman and traveling truck farmer, Paul sees no contradiction in the fact that he ran a *cantina* for years on the same site where his holy shrine is today. And when this longtime Penitente in the Santa Cruz *hermandad* decided he wanted to be a musician, he borrowed instruments from the bands performing in his bar and figured out how to play.

Self-taught on the accordian and the violin, Paul used to play for the Matachines Dance in nearby San Juan Pueblo. He also played *entriegas* at weddings and baptisms, and, of course, sang many an *alabado* at neighboring *camposantos*.

But it is those gaily painted graveyard crosses that Paul Pacheco will be best remembered for when he finally crosses the line between life and death and, like Christ in an illuminated wagon, rolls fearlessly into another dimension.

REID EVANS

eid Evans still has his vintage F-100 Ford pickup parked outside his hundred-year-old adobe with its incongruous canary-yellow fiberglass portal. He bought that truck for $175 years ago in Los Alamos. Got 195,000 miles on her now, but still purrs like a kitten when he starts her up in the morning.

At seventy-seven years of age, Reid is a lot like that truck. Plenty of mileage on those bones, but everything's still in running condition. And though the odometer is on its second trip around, Reid's ready to start all over again.

Everybody knows Reid in these parts—he's got a smile and a wave for young and old alike. Got plenty of girlfriends, too, to hear him tell it, and there's a lot more young ones than old. But Reid loves them all, and not just the women who give him gifts and pose in photographs with their arms draped affectionately around his aging shoulders. Reid just plain loves everyone.

An R-rated Dale Carnegie, Reid likes to press the flesh, invite you in, share a laugh. "Smile and they'll smile back; love 'em and they'll love you back"—that's his motto, and he lives it with flat-out ebullience.

Of course, he's got more of a chance to do that these days, since he's not working any longer, naturally, and he's divorced now too. No animals on the place anymore to hold him down either, and he's never been happier.

"First thing I do in the morning is get up and take a bath. I get dressed right away and I'm ready to go," says Reid, whose closet reveals a wild array of outfits. There's a pair of scandalously pink designer pants hanging there, as well as a fine leather coat with early Navajo silver buttons, the coat Reid slips on when he attends the dances at Santa Clara and San Ildefonso pueblos. Here, too, is one of Reid's favorites, a French pink and black see-through shirt. "When I put this one on, I tell all the girls, 'You get a good look, now,' " the septuagenarian says.

The wardrobe Reid has chosen for today is a touch tamer, but no less smart. He sports a nicely tailored white shirt, a large silver bolo tie, and matching silver belt buckle. He's also put on a silver bracelet and wrist cuffs, and then, of course, there's the 24-carat gold cross he always wears on a chain around his neck.

The cross, Reid explains, was a gift from Christine, a girlfriend of his who claimed it was a genuine relic from the Santa María—you know, that ship you read about in the third grade. And you can be as skeptical as you'd like about that claim. Reid will just smile at you until—well, until you smile back.

But there's no doubting the fact that the cross has been a lucky piece for Reid. "I've had the best life any man could have!" he crows, and the evidence is all around him. Reid, you understand, doesn't just wear relics around his neck; he lives among them in a house full of antiques and memorabilia that tell his life story with alternating understatement and flamboyance.

Reid's biography is tied up with the country's railroads, and one of his most prized possessions is the early telegraph machine he has set up on an antique desk. "My daddy taught me on this set," Reid says, tapping out a message. Reid's father, a "short Welsh-man," as he describes him, started work with the Wabash Line in Illinois. But when Reid was still a boy, his father followed a brother out to Texas, where the climate was warmer and he could find work as a train dispatcher.

"When I was thirteen, I was doing my dad's station work, han-dling the wire," Reid recalls. "But then the flu epidemic came, and the boss told my dad, get Reid out and send him to the next sta-tion. I was the 'relief', going from station to station."

And thus Reid began his thirty-three-year career with the rail-roads. "When I was fourteen, I'd be out playing ball with the kids, and people would come up looking for the agent. They didn't

want to believe I was the agent and could send their telegrams better than anyone else. I wanted to be the best telegraph operator
there ever was, and I accomplished that," Reid says—and he must
have been pretty good at it, for when his supervisor became president of the railroad, he brought Reid along with him to Houston.

After three decades of service with the railroads in Texas, Reid
retired, but he still had a lot of miles left to log. So he climbed into
his pickup and drove north from El Paso, eventually pulling into
the Santa Fe Plaza. "As soon as I saw the plaza, I said, this is for
me," Reid remembers. After a brief stint selling real estate in the
capital, he purchased an apple orchard in Chimayó for $2,800, the
same fertile acreage where he still lives today.

It was after moving to Chimayó that Reid began a new life,
working at a variety of jobs. He started in Los Alamos, expediting
freight and unloading steel. Then he worked at the city ticket office
of the Santa Fe Railroad, after which he was the telegraph agent in
Bernalillo and Rowe. Sometime during these years he worked as a
night auditor at La Fonda de Taos, and he managed to sell a few
raspberries on the side as well. Reid also had the first herd of
Nubian goats in this part of the country, and he once raised some
five hundred turkeys, which he butchered and sold door-to-door
in the capital city.

It was when Reid was an office manager in Los Alamos that the
aging bachelor met his wife. Met her over the phone, actually. Said,
you've got a nice voice—you from Texas? No, Irene replied—she
was from Brooklyn. Meet me anyway in such and such a place in
ten minutes, he replied, and she did and they were married.

Of course, she should've had a nice voice. She was a singer, after
all. Performed with the Rockettes and appeared in the movie *Can-
Can*. "I was married to the greatest singer and sweetheart in the
world," Reid declares, adding in the same breath and without so
much as a shift in tone: "When we got divorced, the judge gave her
everything but the shirt off my back."

Reid's wife, however, gave him a few things, too, including five
children and thirty years of memories, but the geriatric playboy is in
no mood to reminisce about bygone bliss. He'd rather talk about
his gaggle of girlfriends and all those gifts they've been lavishing on
him over the years.

There's that knocker in the shape of a human hand on the front door, a gift from a girlfriend in Houston. And there's the bronze bell he rings in the new year with, a gift from a girlfriend who lives in Paris—Texas, that is. "She wanted me to move in with her on her ranch," Reid says, wondering aloud whether he might not be better off today if he had taken that "pretty cowgirl" up on her offer.

Of course, then he wouldn't have been around to receive some of these other gifts, like the revolving, candy-striped barber pole that reads, "Art Gallery." It still works and, yes, it's a present from another girlfriend, just like the oil painting of Reid himself, one of several portraits executed by yet another girlfriend.

Yet, they're not all gifts from the fairer sex—Reid himself has collected many of the antiques that surround him in his home, like those brazed copper kettles he picked up from the old San Juan Mercantile, the landmark general store that was a center of commerce in the north during the early years of the century.

Reid has an antique scale with brass weights he found in a Lebanese candy shop in San Francisco, and a lobster trap he traded for a collection of doorknobs. There's also a large triangle from Red River, an ancient mailbox from the Santa Cruz post office, a butter churn, a pair of sheep shears, a French heater, a turn-of-the-century bicycle wheel, and the tether and hooks off an ice wagon from a tiny town in Texas. A polished wooden pitchfork once used to feed Connecticut racehorses hangs over a tiger-maple cradle that Reid purchased for $15 at Tennessee Ernie Ford's home.

And, in what Reid identifies as the "Queen's Room," is his prized Jennyland daybed. "It's the only one in a double I know of," he says as he stretches out on the bright red bed. But he's only on the bed long enough to strike a Playgirl pose for a photograph, and then he's up again, showing off his collection of meerschaum pipes, complete with a wrought iron set of ember tongs dating from the 1750s.

There are countless other objects in Reid's collection, including even a couple of well-preserved outhouses in the yard, but it's his railroad memorabilia that have the greatest meaning. Things like a train order-hook that still works as well as it did when Reid used to send tickets rolling through the Santa Fe office, or the impression press from Watrous that the railroad company has been trying to purchase from him for years.

"We used these in the days before carbon paper," Reid says,

gesturing to the red machine with the legend, "Wells Fargo and Company, 1857."

"All the reports in those days were written in indelible pencil. We'd put a tissue with a damp cloth over the report and leave it in the press for a few hours, and that would leave a record."

Reid, too, has left an impression on all those people he's smiled at and laughed with and loved. "I'm only a sixth-grader, but I've got a Ph.D. in living," he says. "You can close your story with that."

And I will, for Reid Evans has surely earned his degree.

AGUEDA MARTÍNEZ

"*Yo todavía bailo en el telar,*" says Agueda Martínez, dancing at her loom on a crisp morning in her eighty-third winter. The pale light of a breaking sun weaves through the window of her adobe home in Medanales, illuminating the clutter of the room—the assortment of rachets, rods, and reeds leaning against the whitewashed wall; the mountain of rags in the corner that will be cut into strips, twisted on a *malacate*, and woven into intricately designed *sarapes*; and the ancestral cast-iron heater crackling with the cedar the *anciana* herself split even earlier in the morning.

The calendar at doña Agueda's side is more than a decade out of date, but time here is not measured in years but, rather, in the rhythmic beat of the huge *telar* itself as it creaks and groans on its hand-hewn gears, responding to the weaver's deft two-step. It's a mesmerizing rhythm, like that of a cradle rocking on a blood-hardened mud floor, or a timeworn hoe biting musically into the soil. It's a rhythm laid down by those early *pobladores* who dug the original ditches and built the first looms in this land; it's the rhythm doña Agueda still lives by, in spite of the twentieth century.

And the modern world has come knocking at doña Agueda's door. A legend in her own time, doña Agueda is probably the best-known weaver in New Mexico. She's the recipient of the first Governor's Award for Excellence in the Arts and the subject of a Moctezuma Esparza documentary nominated for an Academy Award. Her work has been featured in countless exhibitions at galleries and museums throughout the nation, including a show at the Smithsonian Institution. Yet, the fiercely independent *anciana* hasn't yielded an inch to the fame and recognition. She still leads the traditional life of her *antepasados*, and it's a *modo de vivir* that's anything but quaint.

"*No me hace trabajo jalar agua de mi noria,*" she says, and though it may not seem like work to doña Agueda to draw water from her hand-dug well and haul it inside, bucket by bucket, it's only because she's *impuesta*—used to a life of relentlessly hard labor. The *anciana* also uses the phrase *no me hace trabajo* to describe her use of *el escusado de afuera*, her outdoor toilet. Of course, it *is* work on such icy mornings as these to walk the hundred yards to her outhouse, but the elder has done so all her life and sees no reason to stop now, especially since she's convinced it's healthier than staying indoors. Anyway, as doña Agueda puts it, "*Los gringos lo tienen al revés*—they go outside to have their picnics and come inside to do their *necesidades.*"

Cooking with gas or electricity is another contemporary practice doña Agueda finds unnatural: the *frijoles* just don't come out as *sabrosos* as those that are cooked over a wood fire. Though that means the *viejita* must wield an *hacha* to chop her own firewood, it's those very *quehaceres,* those daily chores that she credits for keeping her strong and *saludable.*

And self-reliant. Doña Agueda doesn't worry about a power outage or a break in the water lines; she produces everything she needs and uses everything she produces. As she points out in one of the most memorable scenes in the Esparza documentary, she even puts her old shoes to good use after they're worn out: "I just throw them in the fire and make a tortilla with them."

The *anciana* has, no doubt, made plenty of tortillas with her *zapatos gastados* over the long years of her life, for she has never been one to remain idle. "*Mientras que yo pueda, yo me voy a mover,*" she says—"While I'm able to do it, I'm going to keep moving," and the place she most loves to move in is her *huerta*. For over half a century, the "garden" for doña Agueda has meant a large patch of vegetables, an even larger stand of the blue corn she roasts and grinds to make her own *atole* and *chaquegüe,* and a massive plot of chile—enough to produce a pungent green mountain in the *despensa* and rows of *ristras* ringing the portal. It's a vision of *riqueza*—these fiery chains of chile hanging under the eaves of the tin-roofed adobe—but that picture-perfect image is the result of long hours of labor under the blistering New Mexican sun. Still, there's no place doña Agueda would rather be: "What I love the most," she says, "is working outside, under the sun."

What doña Agueda dislikes the most is witnessing the steady erosion of her traditional lifestyle in today's world. *"Se está muriendo todo,"* she complains—"It's all dying out now. *Todo, todo se está acabando."*

"Ya no es como antes—Nothing is like it used to be." *Antes*—what used to be, what came before—is a word charged with meaning for the *anciana,* a password to the past, a time when neighbors lived in peace with each other and in harmony with the land. *"Antes la gente estaba unida,"* doña Agueda says—"In the old days, the people were united."

That bond was especially strong among women, the *viejita* recalls. "All of us women would get together to cut the hay and the wheat. Hundreds of *fanegas* of wheat we'd harvest, and then we'd wait for the wind to come up so we could separate the wheat from the chaff. Sometimes we'd have to wait until late at night. *Y los niños andaban con nosotras siempre*—The children were always right there with us. *Antes no había day-care."*

Doña Agueda dismisses the difficulty of her life as a *ranchera* with a wave of her calloused hand. In fact, the matriarch describes that subsistence lifestyle as beautiful. *"Era muy bonita la vida de antes,"* she says time and again.

Her words, however, are not so effusive when she characterizes *la vida de hoy en día.* "Nowadays, you don't see kids *todo el santo día.* Why? Because they're all sitting in front of the television set!"

In her day, doña Agueda continues, children spent most of the *"santo día"* out in the field with the *cavador.* "I'm not saying we were all *santitos* in the old days, but there was more respect back then. *Ya no hay respeto.* In those days, anyone who was older than you could whip you if you didn't behave. *El vecino sí nos daba fregazos con un güen chicote.* I still keep a whip myself over there for my own *nietos,"* the *viejita* says with a jagged smile.

But she quickly adds that she has no *quejas*—no complaints about her own family—and it's obvious her feelings go far beyond that. "I've had a long life. *Yo creo que mi vida saldría como una biblia*," doña Agueda says. "I think the story of my life would come out like a Bible."

And she does have a family of biblical proportions: six daughters and two sons, some seventy grandchildren, and more than eighty great-grandchildren scattered throughout the nation. Doña Agueda says she has taught them all two things: love of the land and skill with the weaving shuttle. And many of her *hijas, nietos,* and *bisnietos* do weave. Doña Agueda's daughter Cordelia Coronado owns a weaving shop in Medanales, La Lanzadera; another daughter, Eppie Vigil of Alamosa, Colorado, has mastered her mother's art to such a degree that she was chosen for a National Heritage Fellowship.

Unlike her children, doña Agueda did not learn the art of weaving from her parents but, rather, from her late husband. She credits her natural bent for the art, however, to her Navajo great-grandparents. In fact, she says she still has some of the *jergas* made by her *bisabuela,* who was a Navajo captive in the previous century.

Doña Agueda first began weaving for pay in 1921 with Lorenzo Trujillo of Río Chiquito. Then from 1924 to 1959 she produced *sarapes* for the well-known Chimayó and Española trader E.D. Trujillo. Those weavings, of course, sold for only a fraction of what her classic *colonias,* or Río Grande blankets, command today. Yet, doña Agueda still weaves in her traditional style, cutting and twisting rags on a hand spindle to create colorful masterpieces that sell almost before the *viejita* can cut them off her *telar.*

"*Mis sarapes andan por todo el mundo*—My weavings go all over the world," she says; yet just as often the world comes to doña Agueda. Some visitors, of course, make the trek to her peaceful home near the Río Chama not so much to purchase weavings as to simply meet the star of the documentary they've seen at a film festival or in a college course—to watch the gritty *viejita* slapping tortillas in her *cocina* and drawing *ollas* of crystal water from her all too photogenic well. Doña Agueda has a hard time comprehending why.

"*¡Tanto que traen ese mono!*—Such a big fuss they make over that movie!" doña Agueda exclaims. "Just the other day, some people from California came to take my picture. They've already seen this poor face in the show, so why do they want to see it in person, too?"

It's not that doña Agueda is a recluse; it's just that such intrusions interfere with her *quehaceres*. "Sometimes I'll be out in the field hoeing my chile, and I'll have to quit working and walk up to the house to meet people," she complains. "*Si no, pues pasan por mis matas como vacas*—If I don't, they'll come trampling through my plants like a herd of cattle."

Doña Agueda fixes another shot of the weft—formerly a *comadre's* husband's workshirt—shifts treadles, gives the hand-polished beater a couple of hefty pulls, and shakes her head ironically. She's proud of the recognition her work has received—proud of the awards, the exhibits, and, yes, the movie. But she refuses to let anything disrupt the rhythm of her daily life.

And, unless her legs wear out before her famous shoes, doña Agueda intends to go right on cooking tortillas with those *zapatos*, hoeing her chile, chopping her firewood, drawing her water, and dancing on her generational *telar* for many years to come.

PETER GARCÍA

he deerskin drum pounds like a primordial heartbeat. The singer begins a low-throated chant that slowly spirals into a melodic, pulsating song. It's a new song Peter García has composed for the Cloud Dance, yet it tells a timeless Tewa tale about the seasons, the four directions, the colors of nature, and the earth's bounty. It's a song celebrating the natural cycle of life, and the singer himself is at the center of that cycle.

"I heard my dad sing this one way back," Peter says, recalling how, as a teenager, he danced this same Cloud Dance as his father led the chant. Now Peter stands in his father's place, creating and singing the songs that beat at the heart of the Pueblo dances while his own children and grandchildren dance.

Peter's father is gone now, but his legacy lives on in his son. "My dad was a great composer of Indian songs," Peter says of the late José Antonio García. "I guess that's where I got my talent."

One of eleven brothers in a family without a single sister, Peter recalls how his father was always encouraging his sons to listen and learn about the "old ways" of San Juan Pueblo. And listen they did, as evidenced by the fact that Peter and many of his brothers play a central role in the ritualistic life of their native pueblo today.

Though he and his brothers have followed in their father's footsteps, Peter still laments not having done more to preserve the elder's songs and wisdom. "I wish when my dad was still here, these recording machines would have been available," says Peter, who himself only recently recorded some of his own compositions.

"So many of my dad's songs were lost," he continues. "Even our language is going extinct because we didn't listen to our ancestors."

Though he might not be able to recoup what has already been lost, the sixty-year-old singer has spent the better part of the last two decades forging a cultural link with the next generation.

Founder of the San Juan Indian Youth Dancers, Peter has been working since the 1970s with the youth of the pueblo, teaching them the old songs and such traditional dances as the Buffalo, the Eagle, the Butterfly, and the Dog. "The youth group helps keep our culture alive," Peter says, "and it helps keep our kids away from drugs and all that stuff because, if they want to participate, they have to really be dedicated."

Peter himself has long been dedicated—not solely to composing and singing songs for the Comanche, Deer, and Turtle Dances at San Juan Pueblo—but also to being a sort of ambassador of goodwill to all the people of the Española valley. There is hardly a better-known person in the valley, partly because of his eighteen-year tenure behind the meat counter at the old Peoples store, and partly because of his effusive personality and irrepressible good humor.

After serving in the navy during World War II—he still sports several oversize navy tattoos on his hefty arms—Peter married Pueblo potter and embroiderer Reycita García in 1950. Soon after, he began working as a meatcutter during the days at Peoples and taking classes in cabinetmaking in the evenings at Santa Cruz under the auspices of the GI Bill.

"I picked up the Spanish pretty well," Peter says of those years when he worked among the largely Spanish-speaking population of the Española valley. He recalls, for instance, the day a local *viejita* was in Peoples, hunting for something in the cosmetic shelves located next to the meat counter.

"I asked her, '*¿Quiere ayuda?*—Do you need any help? *¿Qué busca?*—What are you looking for?'

"Well, that was the year those deodorant sprays first came out, and the old lady told me, '*Mi hijita quiere ese... ese National Guard*—My daughter wants some of that... that National Guard.'

"Now, *that's* a real story!" Peter says with a bellowing laugh.

After leaving his job at Peoples, Peter became a liaison officer for the Española Public Schools, directing the Native American federal programs. It was at this time that he formed the Youth Dance Group, as well as a chorus group of youth singers that toured the Española schools and neighboring school districts, performing such dances as the Matachines. In the last few years, this grandfather to "only eighteen grandchildren," as he puts it, has been a counselor at the Santa Clara Rehabilitation Center.

But it's his community and religious activities that continue to keep Peter busy. "During the winter months, I'm always at the kiva," he says. When he's not at the kiva, or on the road with the Youth Dance Group, or performing his songs at weddings, funerals, and numerous special occasions, Peter can usually be found umpiring baseball and softball games, or even playing Santa Claus for various Pueblo groups and organizations.

Yet, it's still the songs that are at the center of Peter's world, just as they once were at the heart of his father's life.

"The songs just come to me," Peter says, explaining the creative process he undergoes while composing. "Sometimes when I'm told a dance is going to be performed, ideas will come to me as I'm driving or on a break from my job.

"I'll look out there and see the sun, and I'll start thinking of Mother Nature. After a while, a tune will start coming in, and a story. It's like telling a story in our language."

The stories are the old ones, the legends that transmit the symbols and values of a people. Even the drum itself is part of the unbroken line of transmission. In Peter's living room sits the ancestral drum of San Juan Pueblo. "That drum has been in the pueblo for a long time," Peter says, gesturing at the ancient drum, which he indicates was passed down to him by his father-in-law.

"When he was sick, shortly before he passed away, my wife's dad told me: 'My son, you take care of this drum which has been handed down from generation to generation. Keep it at your house, and whenever it is needed, let the community use it.'"

Peter, of course, promised to do so, and he has been true to his word. Since taking custody of the drum, he has seen two different wrappers replace the original buffalo hide covering.

"We use it for sacred doings in the kivas and for social dances. And we use it whether it's raining or not," Peter says, remembering the time he was singing at a Harvest Dance when a cloudburst hit.

"We kept right on going, but by the time we were done, the drum had a hole in it."

Though new wrappers have replaced the worn ones, the drum remains the same, just as the new songs Peter composes echo the ongoing story of his people.

And as Peter pounds that ancestral drum and lifts his voice in the song for the Cloud Dance, a bank of cottony cumulus billows over the mountains. By afternoon, the rains will come.

ALFONSO ALDERETE

e was in that first band of Europeans to set foot in the wild expanses of the American Southwest, and he was a black man. Yet, more than 450 years after Estevanico left his footprints in New Mexican soil, tourist brochures continue to celebrate the state's "tricultural heritage," as if the blacks among us were somehow invisible.

Alfonso Alderete, however, is far from invisible. Like Estevanico, Alfonso set sail from Cuba, but instead of being shipwrecked on the Texas coast, this twentieth-century black immigrant came rolling into the capital of New Mexico. In the four decades since then, Alfonso figures he's probably met ninety percent of the people in Santa Fe while serving drinks in some of the best-known bars in town. But Alfonso is not just a bartender: he's more like a host welcoming you into his own home. Which is probably why they named a restaurant after him.

"*Está en su casa*," Alfonso says as I take a seat in his home on tree-lined East Palace Avenue, one of the oldest residential neighborhoods in the capital. Mildred, whose smile is as engaging as her husband's, immediately makes me feel I truly am "in my home." And as we begin to retrace the odyssey of their lives, I realize Alfonso's story is really a tale of two.

It's a tale in two languages as well, and though the Cuban natives are thoroughly bilingual, Mildred prefers English, having received her secondary education on her mother's island of Jamaica.

Alfonso, on the other hand, grew up in Cardenas, Cuba, and is more comfortable with the fluent Spanish that rolls expressively off his tongue.

Both came to the United States for personal, not political reasons. Like so many immigrants before them, Alfonso and Mildred arrived on these shores with visions of a better life. "Back then, we *cubanos* thought there was money growing on trees in this country," Alfonso says, recalling that his illusions of milk and honey rapidly evaporated. "We found we had to work very hard here—we were always working and trying to save our money."

Mildred was the first to taste life in the states. She met Chicago native Sonny Johns, who was vacationing at Casa de la Rosa, a Havana guest house where Mildred was employed at the time. Upon his return home in 1946, Johns sent for Mildred, who subsequently followed the family when they moved from Chicago to Nambé. When Johns needed help to maintain his rambling ranch house north of Santa Fe, Alfonso came to work on the *rancho* and to marry his longtime *novia*.

Naturally, the couple has many fond memories of the first two years of their married life at El Rancho de Nambé in the late 1940s, but Mildred, especially, was not accustomed to rural living. "After Havana and Chicago, I just wasn't happy with the darkness and the crickets," she says. And so the couple moved to the capital, where Mildred became a nurse at St. Vincent Hospital and Alfonso went to work tending the polished bar at La Fonda Hotel.

In 1950, they were among only a handful of black families in Santa Fe. And though they suffered some discrimination when they first set out to purchase a home, most of the couple's memories are positive. "Everyone accepted us," Alfonso says, pointing out that many a door was opened to them because of the language they shared with their neighbors, customers, and patients, even though many of those Hispanic *vecinos* were surprised to learn of that linguistic and cultural link. "A lot of people here had never traveled much and couldn't understand how blacks could speak Spanish," Mildred laughs.

But it wasn't simply a matter of language. The Alderetes became such beloved members of their community through their own hard work and easy personalities—and through their respect for others. "*Hemos criado una reputación muy buena,*" Alfonso expresses it—"We've built up a very good reputation here." The affable *cubano* has also built up quite a loyal clientele over the years as well—from La Fonda to the Bull Ring and, finally, to the restaurant that bears his name. Many of those "regulars" follow Alfonso for his special drink, a concoction of rum and other liquors he's baptized the *caramba*. If you're foolhardy enough to down more than one of the volatile *tragos,* the creator of the drink declares, you'll discover just why it's called the *caramba*.

Though the drink is Alfonso's own original creation, he makes no effort to hide the recipe. On the contrary, he's taught scores of bartenders how to make the *caramba* and other drinks as well. Perhaps he's compensating for the fact that when he first started tending bar, Alfonso worked under a boss who refused to teach him anything. "What I know, I've had to learn on my own—out of *necesidad*. I've had to help myself. *Dios sí me ayuda*—God does help me, but I've always had to go halfway. Still, I believe it's better to teach what I know—*enseñar lo que sé*. That way, when I die my knowledge will remain."

That knowledge will remain, like Alfonso himself, in New Mexico. Though he'd like to someday travel to Cuba to visit the family he hasn't seen since 1958, he's wary about what he might find there. "It's changed so much since I was there, and I'm not sure what they'd think of me. I mean, after so many years of living here, I wonder if they'll think I'm an *americano*?"

Only time will tell if Alfonso's *compañeros* will mistake him for a *gringo*—what *is* certain is that the genial New Mexican has often been taken for the late Anwar Sadat.

International travelers, the Alderetes are especially fond of ocean cruises, and have taken several, including one from New York to France on the Queen Elizabeth. But Alfonso will never forget the cruise he and his wife took several years ago to the Bahamas, mostly because the Indonesian crew on the ship was convinced he was the president of Egypt. "When we'd eat at the restaurant, the waiter would pull out my chair, saying, 'Mr. Sadat,' while they'd leave my wife standing there!"

After the assassination of the Egyptian leader, however, the resemblance began to strike Alfonso as more of a liability than an asset. In fact, he considered postponing a planned cruise to Puerto Rico because he was afraid he might trigger rumors that Sadat was still alive.

As it turned out, the trip had to be canceled anyway because of Mildred's illness. A victim of pulmonary fibrosis, Mildred must take oxygen when she exerts herself. Her condition is exacerbated by Santa Fe's altitude, and her doctors, of course, have urged her to relocate. But Mildred and Alfonso could no sooner leave the town they love as their own than the tenth-generation heirs of de Vargas living down the street. "I'd rather take oxygen than leave!" Mildred declares.

Alfonso wholeheartedly concurs. "You go to the large cities and all you find are *locos*. If you say *'buenos días'* to someone, they think you're crazy. That's why, when we travel, I always say there's nothing better than when we come back home."

Yet, "home" itself has been changing in recent years, as tourists and trendsetters pour into the plaza in ever-increasing numbers. "Santa Fe used to be a smaller, friendlier place," Alfonso says— "more like a family. Everybody knew everybody."

This newest wave of immigrants may never know the Santa Fe of the past that they have largely inundated, and they may never experience the apoplectic pleasures of a *caramba*, but one thing they should understand is that the brochures don't tell the entire story. For New Mexico possesses something far richer than a tricultural mix: our heritage is a cultural mosaic that glows with many colors.

JENNY VINCENT

awrence would have been ninety-seven years old tomorrow," Jenny Vincent says, seated under the towering trees at her San Cristóbal ranch not far from the mountain site where the English author's ashes are enshrined. Jenny has reason to remember D.H. Lawrence's birthday: had it not been for the writer's infatuation with the mesmerizing landscape of northern New Mexico, she might never have known this land that, over the years, has worked its magic on her as well.

What especially captured Jenny's fancy from the very beginning was the robust tradition of folk music in these secluded mountain valleys. A born musician, Jenny had been captivated since her youth by the traditional songs of cultures around the world. But when she arrived in the San Cristóbal valley in the 1930s and discovered the richness and vitality of *la música de la gente*, Jenny knew she had found, not only her home, but the passion of her life.

Jenny's passage to New Mexico was as meandering as a folk melody, beginning with her birth in Northfield, Minnesota, in 1913. One of six children, Jenny had a natural bent for music; by the time she entered junior high school, she had already learned how to play by ear. She went on to cultivate that musical ear, eventually graduating from Vassar with a degree in classical music.

Yet, even while Jenny entertained herself by arranging music for sextets, she felt inexorably drawn to her real love—folk music. It was her mother, Jenny says, who first instilled that enduring interest in popular music. "My mother loved Caruso and John Philip Sousa. One of her favorites and my personal idol was Paul Robeson."

Jenny idolized the legendary black singer, not only for his music but also for his courage in speaking out for his political beliefs during an era when inalienable rights were for whites only. One of the highlights of Jenny's career came in the 1940s when she got the opportunity to accompany Robeson in concert, and she only wishes her mother could have been there to see it.

The renowned folk singer and activist was performing at a rally in Colorado sponsored by the Progressive party for the Henry A. Wallace campaign. "Robeson had a wonderful accompanist, but he was afraid of flying," Jenny says, explaining that when the regular backup musician was unable to make it to a Boulder concert, she was tapped to take his place. The only problem was that Jenny had no chance to practice with Robeson, but the young accordionist knew all the singer's great compositions—"House I Live In," "Water Boy," and "Ballad for Americans." And she still remembers the words Robeson told her when the performance was over: "You certainly gave me a great backup."

But Jenny's memories range farther back—and farther away as well, for the road that led her to New Mexico began across the ocean. Her first husband, Dan Wells, had been a student of the eminent philosopher Alfred Lord Whitehead, and had written his thesis comparing the works of his professor with the novels of D.H. Lawrence. In 1935, Jenny accompanied her husband to Germany, where he planned to continue his philosophical studies at Heidelberg. The couple had brought along a volume of Lawrence's letters and spent four weeks bicycling through Munich and the environs looking up the locations where the novelist had penned the letters.

"At that time," Jenny recalls, "it had only been five years since Lawrence's death, and his memory was still very alive in the people. 'Yes, we remember the English writer with the German wife,' they'd tell us."

The bicycle trip Jenny and her husband took became known as the "Lawrence trek" when later travelers duplicated it. But the most important upshot of that first trip was the contact the couple made with Frieda Lawrence's older sister, Elsa von Richthofen. Elsa von Richthofen, Jenny notes, also had another famous relative: she was first cousin to the notorious "Red Baron."

Jenny and her husband visited frequently with Elsa von Richthofen during their stay in Germany, which was cut short by the rise of Adolf Hitler. "The political situation was getting too rough," Jenny says. "The women who ran the inn where we were staying were anti-Hitler, but you didn't talk politics."

So Jenny packed up the old twelve-bass Hohner accordion she had toted along with her on the bike, and the couple voyaged to England. In the meantime, Elsa von Richthofen had written her sister Frieda in New Mexico about the young couple who had such a consuming interest in her late husband's work. As a result of that correspondence, the widow of D.H. Lawrence wrote Jenny and her husband in March of 1936, inviting them to visit her at the ranch above San Cristóbal.

Naturally, the couple accepted the invitation, spending an idyllic ten days in the summer of 1936 with Frieda and her new husband, Angelino. Jenny, like the English writer before her, fell in love with this land. One afternoon later that same summer, Jenny and her husband rented horses from Dorothy Brett and went riding up the valley with Diego Arellano, a San Cristóbal native who worked for Frieda. The group came upon an abandoned log cabin that Arellano indicated was for sale. And by February of the following year, the Wellses had purchased the sixty-acre ranch, complete with ranch house, saddle house, and ice house, for $2,500.

During the summer of 1937, the couple renovated the house, after which they decided, as Jenny recalls, "It was too nice for just the two of us." Her husband, who had been teaching at a private school in Massachusetts, suggested bringing some of his students out to New Mexico, and the following summer they began an annual summer camp with six boys from Concord. It was, as Jenny describes it, a "work camp." Students took care of the horses, milked the cows, made adobes, and took cultural trips to such events as the Gallup Indian Ceremonial.

Then, in the fall of 1940, the couple turned their camp into a year-round school, serving both East Coast residents and local students. The underlying principle of the school was to challenge students with a college-prep curriculum while, at the same time, instilling that work ethic established in the original summer camp. "Kids whose families paid for the schooling actually did more work, but they looked upon it as a privilege," says Jenny, who, having grown up in a well-to-do household herself, had come to learn the value of self-sufficiency in this land where people have always had to do for themselves.

It wasn't long before the young folk singer had to apply those living skills, for the outbreak of World War II took away the school's faculty, including Jenny's husband. With only her sister-in-law and one "4-F" man to help her, Jenny took care of her two-year-old son, Larry, and managed the ranch that was without running water or electricity in those days. Farming, which had become a serious part of Jenny's survival, also served as the focal point of her singing career as she began to get involved in the organization of local chapters of the Farmers Union in the rural north. She sang at meetings called by Fr. Glenn Patrick Smith, a Questa priest who was active in the Farmers Union, and she performed at the Rocky Mountain National Convention of the union.

Jenny also shared her singing talent with children. A teacher in Questa, who had collected some of the Spanish folk songs documented during the WPA project of the decade before, invited Jenny to teach some of the traditional *canciones* to her students. "Spanish was not allowed in the schools in 1945, but the teacher said she didn't care if she wasn't supposed to do it—she wanted her kids to have their heritage," Jenny recalls.

As the war drew to a close, Jenny traveled to New York, where she immersed herself in the national folk music scene, singing at hootenannies with Brownie McGee and Tom Glazer. She also worked with the American Theatre Wing and did volunteer performances in military hospitals, including two Atlantic City hotels that had been converted into special hospitals for amputees.

When her husband came back from the war, he decided to stay in the city, but Jenny was yearning to return to her home in the New Mexican mountains. Consequently, the couple was divorced and Jenny settled again in San Cristóbal, but she didn't stay hidden at the ranch. She began, as she says, "to think more seriously about my career," performing at regional concerts, including one at the University of New Mexico in 1948 with Pete Seeger and Manuel Archuleta of San Juan Pueblo.

It was at a concert in Colorado that Jenny met Craig Vincent, then director of the Rocky Mountain Council for Social Action. By 1949 she had married Craig, and the couple remodeled the old school building on the San Cristóbal ranch, turning it into the guest ranch they would operate for the next five years. The Vincents' ranch drew many national figures prominent in the social struggles of the early 1950s, a state of affairs that did not escape the wary eye of McCarthyites. Craig, in fact, was called to appear before Senator McCarren's Internal Security Committee to answer accusations made against him by notorious red-baiter Harvey Matusow.

Though history has long since vindicated Craig Vincent and the scores of other courageous men and women who refused to be intimidated by the latter-day witch-hunt, there is a little-known historical fact about the Vincents' ranch that should be recorded: it was the place where the landmark film *Salt of the Earth* was first conceived. In 1951, blacklisted screenwriter and film producer Paul Jarrico was visiting the ranch, where he met Clinton *"el Palomino"* Jencks, a representative of the International Union of Mine and Smelter Workers who was then assisting Local 890 in Silver City in its strike against Empire Zinc. As a result of their meeting, Jarrico and his blacklisted colleagues, Herbert Biberman and Michael Wilson, joined with Mexican film star Rosaura Revueltas and the men and women of Local 890 to create the film chronicling their historic struggle. Making the film, however, was nearly as difficult and dangerous as the strike itself had been, and Craig still recalls calling state police Captain Black to request protection for the film crew and actors when a local mob of vigilantes threatened to run the so-called commies out of town.

The paranoia and hatred have now faded, but the human legacy remains imprinted on the film, just as Jenny's memories of that turbulent era endure in her mind. What she is especially proud of is the fact that the ranch never lost its ties with the local community. In fact, it served as a cultural center during the 1950s. "We'd have a community night once a week when we'd have cultural programs. Everybody would come from the community, and we'd have music and dancing."

Today, Jenny is still playing the old songs, performing with her Trio de Taos, the musical *conjunto* that includes mandolinist Hattie Trujillo and guitarist Nat Flores. The trio has appeared in concerts throughout the Southwest and has cut a record that features such traditional Spanish *piezas* as *la raspa, el chotis, la varsoviana, la camila,* and *la cuna. Música para una fiesta* is distributed nationally and is used in many bilingual programs. That fact is particularly gratifying to the folk musician who continues to serve as a musical resource person for the Taos schools.

"Kids don't hear this music now. Today's music is only designed to make money. It doesn't have the function that folk music once had, to provide news, stories, and entertainment," Jenny says, adding, "I think of myself as a catalyst. I've dedicated myself to emphasizing the importance of the folk music of our area."

It's been half a century since Jenny first followed D. H. Lawrence into this mountain valley. She was immediately taken by its beauty then, but in the ensuing years, Jenny has given much of that beauty back.

PATRICIO CRUZ

osé Patricio Cruz loads his pipe from an economy tin of Velvet tobacco stationed under a portrait of the Sacred Heart of Jesus. *"Bendito sea Dios,"* he says as clouds of smoke billow in the cool darkness of the womblike adobe.

It's a phrase don Patricio repeats all afternoon as if in thanksgiving for every smoke-filled breath he draws. But, then, the *anciano* has much to be thankful for: after all, the God he continuously blesses has blessed him with one hundred years of life.

Don Patricio's senses are fading, but his memory is intact and his faith unwavering. He relights his pipe and begins to speak about this mud-plastered house where he was born a century ago. *"Mi papá se llamaba Desiderio Cruz.* He built this house. It used to be a *sala,* a big hall, but when I got married, I put up a partition. Then, when we adopted our son, I put up another *tabique.* Who knows how old this house is? *Cuando tenía uso de razón, ya estaba aquí*—From the time I had the power to reason, it was already here."

Don Patricio's wife of fifty-six years, Catalina Martínez, died in 1971 in this same narrow house perched on a hill near the *plaza vieja* of Chimayó. "I took care of her. *Aquí la tenía en esta cama,"* don Patricio gestures to the bed he's seated upon. *"La velamos una noche en esta casa y la otra noche en la morada*—We held her wake one night in the house here and the following night in the *morada."*

They're both "homes" to don Patricio: his father's *casa* and the *morada,* for the centenarian has been a Penitente since the turn of the century. During all those years—through world wars, flu epidemics, floods, and depressions—the devout member of the *hermandad* has prayed the traditional *rezos* of the Passion of Our Lord and sung the *alabados* of his ancestors. For the last eighty years don Patricio has joined his *penitente hermanos* during *Semana Santa,* and he hopes to hear the *pito* echoing off the *peñascos* in this year's Good Friday procession as well; but that depends upon whether he can find someone to take him to the *morada.*

It's a dependency the proud *anciano* doesn't much care for. "All I do is eat now. I can't work anymore. I can barely make it to the corral. I can't do anything now," he says—"*Ya no puedo hacer nada.*"

Of course, that's not entirely true. Don Patricio still prepares most of his own meals, builds his own fires, and takes care of his small herd of goats. But he receives help from the family and the *vecinos*, too. "The neighbors come and split wood for me and bring it into the house. And they bring water in, too, because they don't want me to walk down to the *acequia.*"

Yes—don Patricio's house has no water, no plumbing, no *electricidad.* There are no wires, poles, or telephone lines to interrupt the flow of history here. A dusty kerosene lamp is the most modern invention in the house. Though don Patricio's neighbors keep an eye on him, and his three granddaughters come down from Albuquerque to visit—"*a darme vuelta*," as don Patricio puts it—his life is principally solitary now. "*Yo estoy solo*," he says—except for his *cabras,* of course, the goats he's cared for his entire life and which he credits for his longevity.

"All my life I've drunk goat's milk. I still do now whenever I'm able to milk them. I think that's the reason I've made it so far. I know a lot of people don't like it, but goat's milk is very good for the health—*muy saludable.* But they sell it so expensive now in the store."

Don Patricio once sold his goat's milk, too, but certainly not at such exorbitant prices. The goats themselves sold for less than what a quart of the *leche* costs today. "*Una cabra valía un peso, peso y medio, y un cabrito cuatro reales,*" the elder recalls—"A full-size goat sold for a dollar, a dollar and a half, and a kid went for half a buck."

Along with the milk they provided, don Patricio's *hatajo* of goats, which once numbered as many as two hundred and fifty, served another essential function in those premechanized times.

They were put to work creating *eras.* These threshing floors were made by wetting a plot of earth and repeatedly driving a herd of goats over the area. The hooves of the animals packed the dirt until it was as hard as concrete. Such a durable surface was necessary so the kernels of wheat would not be buried when a team of horses walked over the grain to thresh it.

Don Patricio's *cabras* have not been his entire life, however. In his youth, he worked for many years in lumber mills. "I worked everywhere," don Patricio recalls. "Pagosa Springs, Dulce, Grand Junction—when I wasn't working in one place, I was in another. And then, when I got too old to do that kind of work, I herded sheep for a while."

Finally, he returned to his home to live as his father before him—with his animals, his land, and his faith.

Would we like to see his *santos?*—don Patricio asks, rising and painstakingly walking to an adjoining *cuarto* with another bed, a cast-iron heater, and a stack of split piñon next to a *mesita* crowded with a family of gessoed saints. The antique-wallpapered wall above is dominated by crucifixes and metal-framed semblances of *santos* both familiar and obscure, as well as a yellowing reproduction of *The Last Supper.* The opposite wall is cluttered with the snapshots and formal portraits of don Patricio's family, and the ubiquitous *Río Grande Sun* is scattered on the floor. Dim light filters through a single dingy window, illuminating the *viejito's* face in clouds of swirling smoke.

"*Mira, están retratando a mis santos,*" he says in an almost child-like tone—"Look, they're taking pictures of my saints. *Bendito sea Dios.*"

But we still haven't seen the goats, and though the *anciano* is tired, he insists on accompanying us to the goat pen, after, of course, he puts on the new black Stetson he received during his recent hundred-year birthday party at the Holy Family parish hall in Chimayó.

And, as he makes his slow but steady way down the hill to the *corralito,* don Patricio remarks that one of his *vecinos* was asking him yesterday about how he was still able to handle his goats. "*El dice que batalla mucho*—He says he has a lot of trouble with his. But I told him, I don't have any problems. I just call them, and they all come back by themselves."

It appears we'll be testing the validity of that statement, for no sooner does don Patricio open the makeshift wooden door of his pen, than his six *cabras* go bounding off, immediately disappearing in the grassy field below. "They're going to the ditch, but there's no water in the *acequia*," don Patricio observes nonchalantly as he inches his way inside the pen to see if there's still some alfalfa in the *pesebre*. The goats don't need any hay right now, but I need to ask the question that's been on my mind since we first approached the *corral* and I noticed the bales stacked up on the roof: How does the *viejito* manage to get the *zacate* down?

The answer is simple—and nearly unbelievable. Don Patricio climbs up a homemade ladder leaning against the precarious perch. "I just hold on to one side of the *escalera* when I go up and when I come down," he says as though such a feat were no more unusual than snaring one of the five *cabritos* that have stayed behind in the pen.

"*Bendito sea Dios,*" don Patricio says as he eases down beside a *canova,* a feeding trough the *anciano* himself carved out of a chunk of cottonwood. With a diminutive kid in his hands and his milky eyes focused on some inner vision, don Patricio looks more like an Old Testament prophet than a citizen of the twentieth century, but wait—the *cabras* are returning, leaping up the hill. "Hey, hey!" don Patricio calls, struggling to his feet as the goats dash single file back into the pen.

And now, with the *cabras encerradas* and the saints preserved inside the camera, there only remains one order of business before we leave: *la bendición.*

"*Que mi Tata Dios les dé buena salud,*" the *anciano* pronounces, calling on the Creator to grant us a blessing—and considering how well don Patricio knows Him, that will surely be a powerful *bendición.*

JESÚS RÍOS

triding past mountains of freshly stacked
piñon in his Santa Fe wood yard, Jesús
Ríos hardly looks like a man as old as this
century. He's solid as that *bloque de leña* he
splits with a single blow of his ax, and
even when he takes a coffee break in his cedar-roofed office attached
to his home, Jesús doesn't remove his work cap. In fact, he'll only
pull off his right glove to shake your hand—no sense taking off both
of his extra large Bear Kat work gloves, not when he's going to be
using them again before long.

Unbent and unretiring at eighty-one years of age, Jesús still cuts
wood and moves earth, still works till sundown. His biblical eye-
brows have turned snowy, but he hasn't changed over the years.
What *has* changed is the city all around him, this new Santa Fe that's
ballooned from a *plaza chica* to a chic place. Located in the very eye
of that whirlwind of change, the Ríos Wood and Freight Service has
been a landmark for nearly half a century at the corner of Canyon
Road and Camino del Monte Sol. And though he's hemmed in now
by galleries, boutiques, antique shops, and fashionable, rambling
homes, he still remembers that older Santa Fe where you knew all
the neighbors, *y los vecinos te daban los buenos días de Dios.*

"*Esta calle pa'cá era pura gente nuestra,*" Jesús says—"All this street
where we are now used to be only our own people. Now, if there are
five Spanish families on the whole street, that would be a lot. Our
people have been selling and selling, and now we've ended up *con la
boca abierta*—with our mouths hanging open."

They've been trying for years to get Jesús to move out, too; one company, in fact, offered him a million dollars for his prime piece of real estate. But Jesús is not about to budge—not for money, and certainly not because some of his well-heeled neighbors think his wood yard is an eyesore in an otherwise elite environment. He has his family to think about, he says—and, anyway, he was here first.

Born in Durango, Mexico, Jesús originally came to this country in the company of his father, who worked for the railroads in Ratón. Jesús grew up as a trilingual child, adding English to his native Spanish, as well as the Italian he learned to speak from his *amiguitos*, whose families had emigrated from Italy.

In 1919, he was drafted and underwent basic training in Deming. He was on his way to Ft. Bliss when the armistice was signed. "They asked us if we wanted to stay in the army, and though a lot of the boys did, I said no. I was still very young, you know, and I wanted to return home."

Home, by then, had become Santa Fe, and it was in the capital city that Jesús met his wife, Teresa, whom he married in 1933. "She was born here on Abeyta Street," Jesús says, adding that the entire street of Camino del Monte Sol was once the property of his wife's *bisabuelos*—her great-grandparents. Jesús credits his wife for his success in life. "*Mi familia ha progresado mucho*," he declares—"My family has progressed a great deal, and my wife has helped me out in every way. *Es muy importante, sabes.* If you don't have the cooperation of your *esposa*, you don't have anything."

The couple has raised five daughters, three sons, and has seventeen grandchildren; their *hijos*—Juan, Rudolfo, and Leon—all work in the family business. "They've never worked for anyone else," Jesús says proudly, noting that he now leaves most of the hard physical labor to his sons.

"*Yo trabajaba catorce, quince horas al día, y no me cansaba*—I used to work fourteen, fifteen hours a day, and I'd never get tired. And if I did get a little tired, well, I'd just sit down and rest for a minute, and there I'd go again. Oh, I used to run right over the top of the snow, *pero ya no*—not anymore."

Yet, it's clear that the vital patriarch is still firmly in charge, and he refuses to retire to an easy chair. "I went to Tesuque today to deliver a load of *leña*," he says. "I do it, you see, just so I won't be sitting around here all day long with nothing to do. *Así me entre-*

tengo, me divierto con mi negocio—That's how I keep myself entertained, by staying busy with my work. I've always worked. *Pudieras
decir que yo he dedicado mi vida al trabajo duro*—You could say I've
dedicated my life to hard work."

That work began during the Great Depression when Jesús
obtained a contractor's license and a permit from the State Corpo-
ration Commission to haul construction materials. Jesús and his
demolition crew tore buildings down and then transported the sal-
vaged materials to construction sites for recycling. "I destroyed the
old penitentiary building," Jesús says, "and in 1952 I threw down
all the houses where the old hospital is now. *En seis o siete meses tiré
ochenta y nueve casas*—In six or seven months, I demolished eighty-
nine houses, all of those houses that used to be around the capitol
building. And I hauled materials up to Los Alamos, too—before
and after the war."

Though Jesús started with hand tools and plenty of sweat, his
sons now operate a fleet of *máquinas*—graders, backhoes, front
loaders, and semitrucks. But the business started, really, with the
sale of firewood, an end of the *negocio* that's seen dramatic changes
during Jesús's lifetime. "We used to get wood from right here on
these hills—*en estas mismas lomas*. In those days, we'd leave at seven
in the morning and be back home in a couple of hours with four or
five cords of wood. Now, you've got to travel 130 miles just to find
wood. *Más antes había mucha leña*—There used to be a lot of wood,
but not anymore. Too many people now—*mucha gente.*"

The decimation of the nearby forest is not the only *cambio* Jesús
has witnessed over the last half a century. "All the people around
here used to have their gardens and their animals. Where the Country Store is, well, there used to be a corral with cattle and chickens.
And over there where they built those low-income houses on San
Francisco Street there used to be three families with *ranchos—los
Montoyas, los Barelas, y los Delgados. Tenían los corrales llenos de vacas*—
Their corrals were full of cattle. They'd slaughter the animals and
sell the meat right there. And what is that place now—a shopping
center!"

Yet the physical changes in the *vecindad*—some of which, of
course, Jesús himself helped bring about with his demolition
business—aren't the most crucial matter. "*Antes uno conocía a todos
los vecinos*, but you don't even know the neighbors anymore," he

says, recalling how some of his favorite *vecinos* were the young ones, the boys who used to work after school for him, chopping and loading firewood.

"In those days, I'd split the wood all by hand, and those boys would come over and help me load it up and deliver it. I'd pay them *cuatro reales*—or sometimes a dollar, and then I'd invite them into the house for a sandwich and a soda. *Estaban muy contentos*— They were very satisfied, and they still appreciate me even today."

One of Jesús's former helpers, in fact, expressed his appreciation for the *anciano* when he defended him in front of the Santa Fe City Council. It wasn't the first, nor probably the last time Jesús has had to face complaints from his neighbors. "Three times they've taken me to court to try and make me move out of here. *Un gringo que compró arriba me quería echar de aquí*—A *gringo* who bought property up above here wanted to get me thrown out," Jesús says, bringing to mind the old Spanish *dicho*: *"La gallina de arriba siempre caga a la de abajo*—The top chicken always defecates on the one below." But, that "top chicken" has been unable to run Jesús off his place, and he certainly hasn't caused the *chistoso* elder to abandon his principles.

"My wife and I have taught our children to respect all people, regardless of their race. If a person respects you, then you should also treat him with dignity," Jesús says. It's an old belief, one born in less complicated times when the *calle pa'cá* was filled with familiar faces. It's the belief Jesús still lives by with stubborn good humor and unyielding pride.